Praise fo

This book is a wonderful ex~~~ ~~~~~~~~~~ity
and practical advice are nov ~~~~~~~~~~~~~~~~ Jared and
Becky Wilson have brought together biblical wisdom, theological
reflection, and practical experience to deliver the reader wise and
sound council on variegated topics—ranging from friendships,
money, marriage, the local church, and more. This book reminds
readers that who God is and what He is doing in the world impacts
every facet of our life, and the Wilsons are the right couple to draw
our attention to this cosmic reality.

RONNI KURTZ
Assistant Professor of Theology at Cedarville University and
author of *Fruitful Theology: How the Life of the Mind Leads to the
Life of the Sou*l

Go Outside is a treasure trove of wisdom for all present, future, and
even former twentysomethings. It is filled with wit, written from
a loving heart, and has the markers of battle-tested wisdom from
years of serving this age group. The Wilsons also excel at blending
practical advice with sound theology. Some chapters address the
complex relational nuances of early adulthood (finding a mentor,
being the only young person in a church, wanting to be married)
while others plumb the depths of crucial doctrines and apply them
to the Christian life.

TONY MERIDA
Pastor, Imago Dei Church, Raleigh, NC

Hope this works—I remember my twenties and desperately wondering where I could find a manual on "How to Live Life," and Jared and Becky have managed to write something that's pretty close to a true guide. This book is full of gospel-fueled truths, practical advice, humor, and real-life applications for not just young adults but anyone who has the pleasure of reading it. Hand this out to your kids, your graduates, your grandkids, your friends, and maybe spend some time in it yourself for a good dose of wisdom for life.

ANDREA BURKE
Director of Women's Ministry at Grace Road Church

Jared and Becky have given us a blueprint for the well-lived life that manages not to read like a religious rulebook but a hopeful, Jesus-centered vision for how to get the most joy out of the life God has given. It's clear, honest, taut, and to the point. I can't wait to share it with folks!

JIMMY NEEDHAM
Singer-songwriter, speaker, and pastor

Jared and Becky draw from years of life and ministry to offer sage wisdom for the emerging generation. Humorous and instructive, but full of gospel-driven encouragement, *Go Outside* should be dropped into the hands of teens, students, and young adults who desire godly, but never preachy, insights for the soul.

RONNIE MARTIN
Lead Pastor of Substance Church in Ashland, OH, and coauthor of *Pastoring Small Towns*

As one who considers myself to be very indoorsy, the title of Jared and Becky Wilson's new book felt like a personal attack. In all seriousness, I have always considered Jared to be the gospel-centered Yoda, and with the wit and wisdom of Becky as the coauthor, I am grateful the gospel-centered convictions are being applied to very practical life to help a generation of young adults live a life that brings glory to God and flourish. "While you have the energy, use it to serve and to love," the Wilsons tell us in the book, and we need a generation of Christians to take this call seriously. This book is fun, honest, practical, serious about the gospel, and directed toward a demographic often overlooked in Christian conversation. I'm excited to have our twenty- and thirtysomethings in our church read it together in small groups.

DEAN INSERRA

Pastor, City Church Tallahassee; author of *The Unsaved Christian*, *Getting Over Yourself*, and *Pure*

Jared and Becky have poured valuable wisdom into these pages with authenticity, transparency, and biblical accuracy. The next generation needs to look to their example because they show us how to look to Christ in practical and relatable ways. I can only wish that this book was written when I was in my twenties, but find great joy that countless lives will have this godly insight for one of the most foundational seasons of life.

COSTI HINN

Teaching Pastor, Shepherd's House Bible Church; founder and president, For the Gospel

As the parent of two teenagers, I've learned that if someone besides me tells them the same thing once that I have told them one hundred times, they actually listen to the other person. So thank God for those other people! In *Go Outside*, Jared and Becky are those other voices who share clear, blunt, biblical, practical wisdom for young people in the vein of Proverbs and Ecclesiastes. They point young people to Jesus with actionable, encouraging steps. I am eager for my daughters to read this book and to get it in the hands of young adults at our church to help them live faithfully for Jesus.

BARNABAS PIPER
Pastor and author

GO OUTSIDE

& 19 OTHER KEYS
TO THRIVING
IN YOUR 20s

JARED C. WILSON & BECKY WILSON

MOODY PUBLISHERS

CHICAGO

Unless otherwise indicated, Scripture quotations have been taken from the Christian Standard Bible®, Copyright © 2017 by Holman Bible Publishers. Used by permission. Christian Standard Bible® and CSB® are federally registered trademarks of Holman Bible Publishers.

Scripture quotations marked (ESV) are from the ESV® Bible (The Holy Bible, English Standard Version®), copyright © 2001 by Crossway, a publishing ministry of Good News Publishers. Used by permission. All rights reserved. The ESV text may not be quoted in any publication made available to the public by a Creative Commons license. The ESV may not be translated into any other language.

Published in association with the literary agent Don Gates of The Gates Group, www.the-gates-group.com.

Edited by Connor Sterchi
Interior design: Brandi Davis
Cover design: Erik M. Peterson
Cover illustration of sloth copyright © 2022 by Turaev/Adobe Stock (184735072). All rights reserved.

Library of Congress Cataloging-in-Publication Data

Names: Wilson, Jared C., 1975- author.
Title: Go outside... : and 19 other keys to thriving in your twenties / Jared and Becky Wilson.
Description: Chicago : Moody Publishers, 2023. | Includes bibliographical references. | Summary: "Go Outside...And 19 Other Keys to Thriving in Your Twenties"-- Provided by publisher.
Identifiers: LCCN 2022038700 | ISBN 9780802428264
Subjects: LCSH: Spiritual life--Christianity. | Well-being--Religious aspects--Christianity.
Classification: LCC BV4501.3 .W55467 2023 | DDC 248.4--dc23/eng/20221228
LC record available at https://lccn.loc.gov/2022038700

Originally delivered by fleets of horse-drawn wagons, the affordable paperbacks from D. L. Moody's publishing house resourced the church and served everyday people. Now, after more than 125 years of publishing and ministry, Moody Publishers' mission remains the same—even if our delivery systems have changed a bit. For more information on other books (and resources) created from a biblical perspective, go to www.moodypublishers.com or write to:

Moody Publishers
820 N. LaSalle Boulevard
Chicago, IL 60610

1 3 5 7 9 10 8 6 4 2

Printed in the United States of America

For our daughters, Macy and Grace

Contents

Introduction

(Jared)

My favorite movie when I was ten years old was *Back to the Future*. It remained my favorite movie for a long time, all through my high school years. Even if you haven't seen it, you're likely familiar with the basic plot: Marty McFly finds himself in Doc Brown's DeLorean time machine going back to the 1950s and, after some inadvertent mishaps, must make sure his teenaged parents fall in love in order to save himself and his family. The main idea of the movie, it seems to me, is that the hero must preserve the past to preserve the present. But as Marty discovers in the end, changing the past doesn't just preserve the present, it improves his future.

This book is our DeLorean. Of course, it's a lot cheaper. And it's not as cool. (You aren't as likely to impress your friends toting this thing around as you would cruising around in that sweet ride.) But we're looking at this project a bit like that DeLorean. It is a time machine thought experiment of sorts, imagining how we might change the past to improve the future.

Becky and I have been married now for twenty-seven years, and we've learned an awful lot about relationships, largely through making plenty of mistakes along the way. We have two college-aged daughters, and we've learned a lot about parenting in all our years of raising our girls, largely through making plenty of mistakes along the way. We have served in ministry for thirty years now, and we've learned a lot about grace and spiritual growth by—you guessed it—making a lot of mistakes!

I once heard a preacher say he found the land mines in his church by stepping on them. That really resonates with me!

So we imagine: If we could go back and intervene in our past, if we could talk to our younger selves, what would we say? What advice would we give ourselves?

We got a chance to think intently about this when the student leadership staff at Midwestern Seminary and Spurgeon College in Kansas City, Missouri, asked us to come give a talk to students on what we wish we'd known when we were their age. Becky and I each made a list of three things, and we took turns talking through each item. That project blossomed into this book.

We enjoy a great life today, and we work hard in the present at making sure our future is oriented around the things of God, the things that matter most and matter eternally. But that doesn't mean if we could go back we wouldn't help ourselves avoid some of those land mines. That's what we want to do for you.

So we want you to get in this poor excuse for a DeLorean and go for a ride with us. Along the way, we'll offer some hard-won advice from the trenches of real life. And we'll listen to some of the biblical writers who had a chance to counsel younger people they were discipling and mentoring, including at least one speaking to his younger self.

Back to the Future is just a movie, of course, and a fantasy movie at that. None of us can change our pasts. But we can help you preserve your present and even improve your future.

Now, I've often thought about what my past self would do if my present self could go back and talk to him. I would really want my past self to listen to the me from the future. But if I'm honest, despite the desperate need I would have to avoid so much I'd be warning myself about, I'm a little worried that I wouldn't really listen.

How about you? Are you listening?

Don't wait until you "have time" to develop healthy habits

(Becky)

It's easy to believe that once you graduate, get married, get a better job, settle down, or [insert whatever other milestone you're hoping to reach next], you will have more time to focus on Bible study, prayer, and other spiritual disciplines. Quite the opposite is true. For most people, responsibilities and time-consumers will not decrease as you grow older—at least, not until you have retired and all of your children (if you have them) are grown. Even then, if you are well connected with a church family, you will likely realize that your calendar can easily stay overpopulated in every season of life. This is not necessarily a bad thing, but it does mean you need to develop healthy habits now for staying grounded in Scripture, focused on the gospel, and engaged in ongoing conversation with the Lord through prayer.

Just a couple weeks ago, Jared and I delivered our youngest daughter across the country to Lancaster, Pennsylvania, where she attends college. Currently we're on week six of being "empty nesters." But man, that nest stays buzzing.

We have lived through many seasons of life, all of which I think we somehow assumed would become at least a bit less busy than the ones before and all of which were not at all less busy, including this one. At this very moment I am typing in a hotel room many, many miles from home, where Jared is speaking at a conference, and we will catch another plane in a couple days to fly to a different location many, many miles from home so that he can do it again. And then we will do this about five more times over the next six weeks or so, staying home just long enough to unpack, do some laundry, and repack.

To be clear, it is our choice to travel together in this season of life as much as possible. We have spent a great deal of time apart over the last ten years as Jared has traveled to preach and teach and I have stayed behind to care for our daughters and our home.

Now that both of our girls are grown, I am able to join Jared much more often without shirking any major responsibilities at home, so I'm thrilled to be able to join him on the road, but this doesn't exactly provide long stretches of quiet time in Scripture on a regular basis. It would be easy to look at my current calendar and see that most of my busyness is optional and that I could have much more free time in my schedule if I chose to. And that would be true. But that's kind of the whole point.

Almost all of us could create more quiet space or downtime in our lives if we really wanted to. But almost all of us fill those quiet spaces and downtimes with activity of some kind. The key is to make sure we prioritize behavior that is necessary for health and wholeness before we begin adding layers of voluntary busyness over a schedule that is already full. This of course will look different for everyone, and there's no need to compare ourselves with anyone else.

In this season of frequent travel for me, this looks like reading or listening to Scripture and theology in airports and on airplanes. And choosing not to tune out while Jared is speaking, even if it's a message I've already heard several times. (Can't we all use frequent reminders?) I wish I had more time to sit on my big comfy couch at home with a cup of coffee in one hand and my Bible in the other. I wish I could worship with my church family in Missouri more often. But this is not the season for that. So I desperately need personal spiritual disciplines that will keep me grounded in Scripture and consistently communicating with the Lord. And so do you.

> It's best to get serious about our spiritual lives now so we'll be prepared with a steady discipline that can be our lifeline for every season.

Maybe you're thinking you'll get "really serious" about these things once life settles down. When you're settled at school. When you've graduated. When you finally land a job and land a spouse and land the life you've always wanted.

But the truth is, you will always come up with reasons why spiritual disciplines can wait. And every stage of our lives comes with its own unique busyness. It's best to get serious about our spiritual lives now so we'll be prepared with a steady discipline that can be our lifeline for every season.

So, whatever it is that keeps you busy these days—traveling, working long hours, or studying late into the night—there are creative ways to nourish your soul through prayer and the intake of Scripture. Here are just a few suggestions for incorporating spiritual disciplines into your life, even if you think you have no time for them:

- Instead of picking up your phone to scroll through social media as soon as the alarm goes off, first open your Bible (or even a Bible app on your phone) and read for just five minutes. In a year's time, that's over thirty hours of reading in just five minutes a day, which is enough to read through almost half of the Bible!

- Invest in an audio Bible app. They are wonderfully inexpensive. My favorite is the Dwell Bible app, which is about the cost of one cup of coffee per month. Listen to it while you get ready in the morning, while you commute, while you exercise, while you cook or do chores, or even while you shower if you have some water-resistant earbuds. I suspect you will be surprised at just how much these little moments will add up. But even if they are much briefer than you would like, you will still be developing a habit. And this isn't a race. There is no deadline for getting through Scripture within a specific timeframe. The goal is simply to take it in on a regular basis, no matter how small or large the quantity. It's a rhythm of life that always includes a desire for Scripture intake we're after here, not a begrudgingly completed checklist of verses for the day.

- Make it a habit to pray every time you are preparing a cup of coffee (or scooping up a bowl of ice cream, or . . . you get it, whatever you do somewhat habitually that doesn't require a lot of brainpower so that you can focus your thoughts on prayer). It might seem almost silly at first since these moments feel so brief, but I firmly believe you will find yourself craving these encounters of intimacy with your Savior and looking for ways to extend the time you spend with Him. Again, quantity is not as important as consistency. The hope is that these regular conversations with your Creator and Comforter and Provider and King will become so satisfying that they will lead to a desire for more. But if you wait until your lifestyle is magically so flexible and relaxed that you can comfortably dedicate hours to prayer every day, you will likely never start the conversation.

- Go to church regularly. Busyness can make it awfully easy to excuse ourselves "just this once." And then "well, maybe just until this paper is finished." Or "just until after finals." "Okay . . . definitely once this semester is over." The enemy will always try to provide you with excuses to stay home from church. Don't buy the lie. Attending and serving in a local church develops spiritual depth and disciplines that are difficult if not impossible to gain any other way.

- Pray through stress. I know, you don't "have time." But I fully believe that even a ten-second prayer whispered in desperation can have a greater impact than you might believe. If you ask the Lord to help you find ways to spend more time with Him, He will help you. Try it. From now on, every time you're running a little late or leaving home frustrated because you didn't have time to read your Bible or pray, just speak a quick prayer, "Lord, help me find ways to spend more time with You!" Do this once, twice, three times a day. I promise He will answer.

I could list several more ideas, but since everyone's life is so different, my hope is that this will stir up your own thoughts about how to personally find ways to seek the Lord in prayer and immerse yourself in Scripture as close to daily as possible. Whatever you think you might lose in less time with friends or movies or games or work or exercise, the Lord will richly redeem in the most life-changing relationship you will ever know and the greatest education you will ever receive.

2.

Use the energy you have while you have it

(Jared)

I vividly remember the exact moment I got old. My first mistake was accepting a friend's invitation to play full-court basketball. I hadn't played any ball in years, but I missed it, and I longed to get back on the court. Back in the day, I was pretty darn good. I was always first or second pick in regular weekend pickup games at the park, and my buddies and I had played in the NBA's touring Hoop It Up tournament when it came to Houston every summer. But years of a sedentary lifestyle were about to catch up with me.

The game started well enough. I was keeping up, trying to get the rust off, mainly passing. You know, just kind of laying low, biding my time. I was huffing and puffing a little harder than I expected, but I was trying to push through.

Then it happened. We were on defense, and one of my teammates nabbed a steal. Direction shifted back up the court, and I was leading the way running toward the opposing goal. My teammate threw a perfect football pass across half court, which landed beautifully in my hands while I was mid-stride. I immediately began dribbling a line of fire up the court, heading to an easy layup.

But it was possible I was not moving as fast as I thought I was. And in my peripheral vision, I could see one of the opposing players remarkably moving across the court faster than I'd ever seen a person move, and before I knew it, he was between me and the goal. As I approached this collision with my defender, my brain was sending signals that felt wonderfully familiar. When you're young and athletic, you don't really even have to think about such things. There's no time at all between the brain sending signals and the body obeying. My brain sent the signal to "fake left and go right." It's something I once did instinctively, smoothly, convincingly.

At this moment, my brain said "fake left and go right," but my body basically said, "Nah, I don't think we're going to do that today." In fact, my body said, "We're probably not ever going to do that." And instead of picking up the move to fake out my defender and dart around him, my legs got confused and instantly locked up. I'm ashamed to tell you that I fell face forward onto the court, and the ball bounced sadly out of my dribble and rolled out of bounds.

One of my buddies came to give me a hand and pull me off the court. "What happened?" he said. I said, "I don't know. But I think I just got old." Another teammate very helpfully said to me after the game, "If it matters, I could tell you used to be good." That was a cold comfort.

I think about this moment a lot, especially since I'm significantly older now than I was then! But I mark it as the moment of my reaching the "other side" of the journey of aging. Firmly ensconced now in middle age, I look back at the days of my youth with a lot of warmth—but also a lot of regret.

I feel warmth because I am grateful for the joys of seemingly boundless energy, of the "glory days" of legendary games of weekend football and basketball with my friends, of feeling like the world was brimming with possibilities and I was brimming with potential. But I feel regret, because I think I squandered so much of those days focusing on things that don't ultimately matter.

If I could go back and talk to myself then, I would say, first of all, "Enjoy this! Enjoy it more than you already are enjoying it." I would tell myself to really cherish the days of youth and all the energy and strength and health that often come with it. Because those days go by so much faster than you think they will. When you're young, time seems to move slowly. But it's really not. And all the abilities of youth are a great gift from God. We should really appreciate them—to the glory of God—while we have them and not take them for granted. Don't let them go to waste in your twenties and thirties. Stay active. Get outside (see chapter 15). Enjoy God's creation. Join a team. Go for regular walks or runs or swims. Don't let your body get lazy or unkempt.

> While you have the energy, use it to serve and to love.

The book of Ecclesiastes is basically the old King Solomon reflecting back on his life with both warmth and regret. He is, in a way, talking to his younger self. He warns his younger self. He encourages his younger self. He longs for young people reading to not make the mistakes he made. And in Ecclesiastes 12:1, he refers to how the "days of adversity come" and the years approach where the pleasures of being young are impossible. And the word of exhortation he gives to the young who so often cannot yet feel or see the approach of the days of "getting old" is this: "Remember your Creator."

While you're still young and have so much energy and ability, remember your Creator. Don't waste these precious gifts on everything but the Lord's business. While you have the energy, use it to serve and to love. Use your youthful energy to repent of laziness and work hard at your studies and your job. Use your youthful energy to go on mission trips. Serve in local outreach efforts. Be a faithful evangelist to your friends and classmates.

I wish that I had spent more of my energy on things that matter more when I had the energy to spend. It's gotten harder as I've gotten older, and in a lot of ways, I have felt like I'm trying to make up for lost time. I have a lot more interest in pursuing a kingdom vision these days but a lot less energy to do it. I don't want you to share this experience.

> You'll never regret investing intensely in the business of His kingdom.

You don't get these youthful days back. Even if you're dedicated to maintaining physical health, make sure not to neglect your spiritual health. Channel your energy that way too. Because, as strong and healthy as you are now, it's going to go away. You won't be young forever. But Christ is yours forever. You'll never regret investing intensely in the business of His kingdom. And your investment *there* is something that will never get old, never decay, never be lost.

Abandon yourself, then, with gusto to the pursuit of Christ's kingdom.

3.

All investments require time to grow

(Becky)

I don't know a single person who would deposit twenty dollars in the bank today and expect to come back tomorrow and withdraw a hundred dollars. And I've never met anyone who thinks you can plant a seed one day and find a fully grown, fruit-filled apple tree a week later. For the most part, we realize these things take time and require work. A retirement fund and a kitchen full of apple pie and cider must begin with a few dollars and a few tiny seeds slowly and patiently given the attention they need to thrive and produce.

Just as these monetary and horticultural investments gain value over time, so do relationships and spiritual disciplines. It is possible, I suppose, for the Lord to do a miraculous work of knitting hearts together quickly, but most of us would agree that the richest and most meaningful relationships happen when friends and loved ones faithfully contribute to each other's lives over the course of many years and especially throughout a variety of seasons. We might greatly enjoy the company of new friends, but we will cling to the trustworthy, tried-and-true long-term relationships when needs and difficulties arise.

This is a natural disposition. It doesn't require much effort to think of our closest friends. They are the ones who show up regularly, the ones we interact with most often, the ones who invest in our lives. But no one becomes that kind of friend just by deciding that's what they want to be and claiming the title. They earn the title by doing the slow, consistent work we just talked about. Showing up. Listening. Helping. Loving. And guess what is required of you if you desire to be that kind of friend and have those kinds of friends? I'll give you two guesses, but you'll only need one.

> You must show up. Listen. Help. Love. Consistently over time, you must invest in the people you wish to call friends.

That's right. You must show up. Listen. Help. Love. Consistently over time, you must invest in the people you wish to call friends. I am sad to report that I know more than a few people who spent their lives mostly focused on themselves and grew to realize later in life that they were lonely. Thankfully the Lord is powerful enough to redeem even this, and I'm grateful to have seen Him do so. But the best way to avoid such a fate is to start early in life and consistently find ways to show people you enjoy their presence.

In much the same way, spiritual disciplines are kind of like old friends. The more we invest in them, the more joy and transformative value they will have in our lives. Consider reading Scripture. It can be a daunting task to open a Bible for the first time, or even for the thousandth time, with very little understanding of what we're reading. But as we gradually and consistently spend time in the Word, as we read in 2 Corinthians 3:18, we are "beholding the glory of the Lord" and therefore "are being transformed into the same image from one degree of glory to another" (ESV). When we come to the Word of God, which tells us itself that it is "living and effective" (Heb. 4:12), with a humble heart and a submissive mind, every encounter with it over time contributes to a deep change within us. This is the power of the living Scripture. So even if you must start

31

with brief moments and scattered thoughts, know that each one matters. Every minute adds to the foundation you are laying to support you for the rest of your life.

I am often still surprised by the way the Lord works through His Word. Having been raised in church and married to a man who speaks and writes and repeats the words of Scripture for a living, I have heard or read most of the Bible multiple times. And yet I am struck by something new every single time. As I grow and learn and fit more of the big picture into place, the details that I didn't understand, and the pieces that had no place to fit the first time I read them, now wonderfully adorn the ever-growing story that the Lord is telling me through His Word. And just like a puzzle gets easier to fill in and more visually appealing with each addition, the story of God's love for us does the same. Every new revelation delivers greater clarity and each moment of better understanding makes it easier to understand the next moment and the next and the next.

I don't know about you, but my favorite friendships are those that feel easier and more comfortable every time we spend time together. So much less work is required and so much more joy is shared once we have laid a foundation of understanding. This doesn't mean we don't continue to put effort into the relationship, only that it feels more natural and comes much more easily each time. Wouldn't you love your time in Scripture to feel the same way? However difficult it might feel to begin this practice, I truly believe it will become more and more natural and easy each time, and my hope is that you will find more and more joy in it as well. Begin this practice now so that even decades from today you can look back with surprise and delight to see the beautiful fruit this investment bears. I can say with confidence that I'm certain you won't regret it.

Porn is more toxic than you realize

(Jared)

I saw my first pornographic images in the fifth grade while riding the bus home from school. A friend had brought one of his dad's dirty magazines. I have forgotten a lot of sexually explicit material I've seen since then, but I still remember those images. I wish I couldn't remember them, but they latched onto my ten-year-old brain and didn't let go. They opened up a Pandora's box of lust and other fleshly curiosity that I spent years trying to destroy, mostly failing.

Here's the thing about porn: if you give it an inch, it will take miles and miles. In Ephesians 4:27, Paul talks about the devil getting an "opportunity." In some translations it says "foothold." There are moments of vulnerability in temptation when we give the enemy just a little bit of ground in our life, and it may not seem like much. It's just a foothold. But he never stops there. If he can get his foot in the door, he will continue to work to push the whole thing open and flood your life with spiritual danger.

> Here's the thing about porn: if you give it an inch, it will take miles and miles.

That's how it is with porn.

When I was in the fifth grade, the internet didn't exist yet. At least, it didn't exist like it does now. And like many young men, I spent my teenage years battling the sin of lust. I sought out pornographic images the only ways I could—late night movies at friends' houses, quick scrolls through dirty magazines at gas stations, etc. Then, in my first year of college, I got my first real computer and had internet access for the first time in my very own bedroom. Like a drug addict, up to this point I was trying to score a "fix" here and there, in alleyways and under the cover of night. Now the drug was piped directly into my room.

Today I know it's even more readily available. You can carry around instant access to things you should never see right there in your pocket or backpack.

Here's what I've learned about porn use from those days and what I would tell myself if I could go back: "This stuff is more toxic than you realize."

I was a Christian back then, so I knew what I was doing was sin. Unlike a lot of unbelievers who use porn, I was ashamed of my habits and desperately trying to keep them a secret. I was awash in guilt and really struggling. It didn't help that I didn't feel like I could talk to anybody about it. To be clear, my sin was my own; I was solely responsible for what I was doing. But I wonder how much pain I could have saved myself—and eventually others—if I believed I could get real, gospel-rich help from someone I could confess to. I would say to myself back then to get help. Take the risk. And I would say the same to you: the embarrassment of asking for help with this struggle is totally worth avoiding the shame of wrecking your entire life later on. Because that's what happened to me.

I gave this stuff a foothold in my life, and it began to take over. I kept it all nice and secret, but sin grows like crazy in the dark. And while I indulged in this secret sin to the point of habit, the outward façade of my being a normal person with a good life became more and more difficult to maintain. Eventually, my secret sin was not content to stay secret. It couldn't be contained in the closet of my private thoughts. Not content to stay confined to a screen, it led me to ruin my own marriage.

See, what we know now about porn use is that it rewires the brain. Neuroscientists have actually discovered this. It dulls our senses, redirects our impulses. We also know that it is directly influential on a host of sexual dysfunctions that are now epidemic in the world. Porn takes what God has designed for a married man and woman and, in the guise of making it more appealing and more exciting, actually makes it more and more boring, less and less satisfying. This is how porn is like a drug. You always need a bigger hit to feel the same high. And like drugs, it can kill you.

The bottom line is that porn *deforms* us. It will make you into someone you never wanted to be.

What we can see happening spiritually, over and over again, is that long-term porn use makes people more impatient and less kind. The continual consumption of images of the objectification and degradation of people made in God's image can't help but result in the user's objectification and degradation of people in their "real life" who are made in God's image.

The use of porn will make you meaner. It will make you a bad lover. It will ruin your ability to share meaningful intimacy with your spouse, including sexual intimacy of course. It can also open the door to a progression of other related problems, as well—cohabitation, divorce, abuse, and other sexual sins you wouldn't have even considered appealing when you started using. The bottom line is that porn *deforms* us. It will make you into someone you never wanted to be. Porn takes something God has designed for our good and the good of others and perverts it to something selfish, harmful, and poisonous.

It took my entire life falling apart to snap me out of my habits. I wish I could go back and stop myself from seeing all the stuff that led to that destruction, starting on that fifth-grade school bus. I can't do that. But what I can do is warn you: porn is more toxic than you realize. It won't just stay in your head. It will crowd out your heart, your home, your relationship with God. You might think you can tame this sin with a little bit of dabbling, but you can't.

So ask for help. Ask God to help you. Ask friends to help you. Sin dies in the light, so bring it out in confession and a request for accountability.

And remember this: the glory of Jesus is so much more beautiful and so much more satisfying than any lurid image you can find on a screen. We know this, because as soon as we're done using that junk, the thrill of seeing something new or exciting immediately gives way to guilt and shame and regret, doesn't it? Remember that, and use that knowledge to intervene in your own thought life by focusing on Christ. The soul cannot abide a fixation with the glory of Christ and a fixation on porn at the same time.

Despite the seemingly all-pervasive poison of pornography, Jesus really does love you. He won't throw you away if you come to Him for rescue. You're not too gross for Him. You're not too dirty for Him. You're not too far gone from Him.

So turn back! Don't be afraid. With the Spirit's help, by God's grace, you can do it.

You will never regret time spent with the Lord

(Becky)

Do you have any friends who know you so well you feel like you can almost read each other's thoughts? Maybe you finish each other's sentences so easily it annoys everyone else. Maybe you can communicate with just a quick glance or a simple hand gesture. Maybe you don't even need that much. Somehow they intuitively know exactly when you need to hear from them or get a quick text of encouragement or receive an invitation to coffee or dinner.

What comfort is the familiarity of well-developed friendship! Here is where we may be the truest version of ourselves—honest about fears and shortcomings, excited about current accomplishments and future plans, relaxed about how we present ourselves (which is to say that we don't even have to think about it). We just *are*, without pretense or premeditated thoughts about presentation.

> The key ingredient to knowing and being known is time spent together. The only way to truly know a person is to be present with them consistently over time.

Now let's talk about what champion gift-givers these kinds of friends are. They know all of your needs and preferences almost better than you do. They know that book you pick up every time you visit the used bookstore together. They know your favorite coffee and chocolate. They know you desperately need a new black sweater because the one you keep wearing is unraveling right before their eyes. And they delight in seeing your joy when they present something to you they know you will use and enjoy.

Have you ever considered how you got there with certain people? It doesn't take long to realize that the key ingredient to knowing and being known is time spent together. The only way to truly know a person is to be present with them consistently over time. To talk and listen. To attentively observe. To "have history" together and understand how their past affects the present. To know each other's character traits and behaviors and how to interpret and respond well to them.

What if I told you that Jesus Christ Himself wants to be that kind of friend to you (except way better)? And here's the thing—He already knows you better than anyone else on the planet, including yourself. You need not make any efforts to reveal yourself to Him. You don't have to worry about whether or not He can handle the real you. You don't need to pretend to be something you're not based on what you think He expects of you. And you certainly don't need to earn His attention or friendship or love. It's already there in glorious abundance.

> How well do you know the Lord? How well do you *want* to know Him?

But relationships have two sides, don't they? Without engagement and commitment by both parties, it isn't really a relationship at all. So here are the big questions. How well do you know the Lord? How well do you *want* to know Him? Do you want to know His voice so well that you recognize it more easily than any other voice? Do you want to receive with joy and gratitude the good gifts He has chosen for you? Do you want to understand His character so well that it naturally shapes yours?

The only way to do these things is to spend time with Him. Consistently. Starting now. Don't waste another day. Hannah Anderson says this about how the Lord reveals Himself: "He doesn't shout His plans from the mountains so much as He repeats them over and over in low, quiet songs that only make sense to those who know the significance of them."* You can know Him in this way by listening to those songs on a regular basis. He desires to communicate with you. He delights in giving you the best gifts you can possibly imagine. He longs to hear your deepest fears and failings and give you grace. He celebrates your accomplishments, but more importantly, He celebrates you. More than any other person you will ever know, He wants you to be the truest version of yourself, the person He created you to be, the person who is most like *Him*.

You have the ability as promised in 2 Peter 3:18 to "grow in the grace and knowledge of our Lord and Savior Jesus Christ." All it takes is a prayer, a few minutes in Scripture, or a conversation with a trusted pastor, teacher, or mentor who can share truth and love. But it takes doing these things consistently throughout

---

* Hannah Anderson, *Turning of Days: Lessons from Nature, Season, and Spirit* (Chicago: Moody Publishers, 2021), 23.

your life. And this is why you won't regret it: every single day of your life you have access to the God of the universe through His Son Jesus Christ by the power of the Holy Spirit, and every moment you spend in communication with Him will transform you. Maybe in the tiniest of increments. Maybe much more slowly than you would like. But so much more powerfully and effectively than any other way you choose to spend time.

To be clear, I am not suggesting that leisure is sinful. I'm a big fan of games and movies and books (including fiction) and laughing with friends. These things are not unimportant. But they are secondary. If the most important relationship in your life is Christ, and you know and understand Him better daily and find your identity in Him, all other areas of life will become more meaningful.

When you reach the end of your earthly life, you will almost surely have forgotten most of the details of how you spent your days. Even the best parts. But "this is eternal life: that they may know you, the only true God, and the one you have sent" (John 17:3). If you know Christ, you will not forget Him. He will be the most incredible friend you have ever known. And He certainly will not forget you. Not only will you carry this relationship and all of its implications into eternity, it's the only way to enter into eternal glory. Spend time with Him now. Every day. Know Him. Love Him. Receive His love. Spend eternity with Him.

6.

Church membership isn't optional

(Jared)

One of the most concerning developments in church life over the last twenty-five years or so has been the virtual disappearance of young adults. Even kids who grow up in church, attending weekly with their families, participating in youth group and other programs, tend to drop out of church when they leave home at a rate of nearly 70 percent.* That's a lot of church kids suddenly deciding church isn't for them!

---

* Aaron Earls, "Most Teenagers Drop Out of Church When They Become Young Adults," Lifeway Research, January 15, 2019, https://research.lifeway.com/2019/01/15/most-teenagers-drop-out-of-church-as-young-adults/.

There are probably a few reasons why this happens. First, for kids who move away from home to go to college, it can be difficult to find a local church that feels comfortable or that resembles the church they grew up in. And some college environments, of course, aren't exactly conducive to a flourishing spiritual life. If you have a new set of peers in a new environment, the value of church may just not be present, and there's no expectation or encouragement to continue a commitment to church.

For others, it's not the new environment of a college campus or new town that makes it difficult but simply the freedom of being a young adult, whether "leaving the nest" or not, making your own decisions apart from parental requirement and family tradition. You're in the season of life now where you get to determine whether your faith is really yours or just a custom handed down by your family. A lot of young people decide that church, at least at this time, just doesn't fit into their own plans for their life.

> The New Testament knows of no Christian faith apart from commitment to the "one another" context of a local church.

Whether you're in college or out, reject the idea that committing to a local church is something only to be done when you're older, more "established," or in the life stage of having a family.

There are a few reasons for this, but the primary reason is because discipleship isn't designed to be done on your own. The New Testament knows of no Christian faith apart from commitment to the "one another" context of a local church. To grow in one's relationship with Jesus, in fact, is to grow in one's relationship with other Christians. And while you can make lots of friends in a campus ministry or other parachurch organization, and even learn a lot in those places that can benefit you spiritually, God's design for optimum growth according to His Word is a local church.

But "God says so" isn't the only reason to commit to a local church even if you only plan to be away from home for four years or less. A healthy local church provides a multigenerational family that is a much healthier environment for growing in wisdom than simply attending a regular program with people your own age. As I said, such programs can certainly be beneficial, but treating them like your church robs you of being around people who have lived longer, experienced more, and have insights and guidance from mileage in their Christian journeys that you don't have.

Certainly, a new church environment, particularly one that has older people in it, may not always suit our stylistic preferences or comfort levels, but consider how even that experience can serve to build patience, empathy, and endurance in you. It does not serve anybody very well spiritually to always have their faith custom-tailored to their own self-interested tastes. We become more like Jesus when we put ourselves in a position to consider and honor people who aren't like us.

There can be a tension point, also, in suddenly finding yourself considering a commitment to a church that feels so different from the weekly attendance of a youth program or a worship service customized to youthful tastes. But remember that you can't do youth group forever! Paul says in 1 Corinthians 13:11 that he put away the things of childhood when he grew up. Part of this for Christians today is not expecting our adult experience of church to carry on the same way as our experience of student ministry, especially if our student ministry programming was conducted in ways quite different from the "big church" we grew up in. This is in fact one of the biggest mistakes churches and youth pastors make—creating an entirely different experience for young people that is pretty much insulated from the

> We become more like Jesus when we put ourselves in a position to consider and honor people who aren't like us.

life of their larger church. Kids raised in youth ministry silos like this usually do not stay in church long after their youth group days are over. The contrast is too jarring. They haven't been prepared to see value in and love the local church, only to enjoy the youth ministry portion of it.

One way you can overcome issues of stylistic preferences and the like in a new church is to commit yourself to serving in some way. How can you help? Maybe you can't change their music or architecture or overall "vibe," but you can selflessly love people and pitch in to help them be the church God has called them to be. There may not be many college students or other young adults there, and there never will be unless someone like you selflessly decides to pioneer that growth!

When I was pastoring a church of mostly older folks in a little New England town several years ago, we were all praying that God would grow our church and grow it younger too. It took a while, but eventually we had one or two twentysomethings decide that it didn't matter to them there weren't a whole lot of others their age in our church. They'd be the first. And then when the next young people visited, they saw people like them. And their number began to increase. But I thank God that one young lady and her brother decided to be the firsts. They took a selfless risk to commit to a church not for its immediate benefits to them but in order to love and bless others. They were the impetus God used to grow our church. So don't turn your nose up at churches that don't have a lot of young people in them. If the gospel is preached there, people believe the Bible there, and people are serious about loving others there, be a pioneer for your demographic. Don't be afraid, as the saying goes, to "be the change you want to see."

> The community of believers is the ecosystem prescribed by God for healthy maturing in the faith.

In the end, we commit to a local church, regardless of our age, because church membership is how God has designed Christian growth to take place. We are individually members of a body (Rom. 12:5; 1 Cor. 12:27). Our faith may be personal, but it's not meant to be private.

The community of believers is the ecosystem prescribed by God for healthy maturing in the faith. Don't use whatever new-found freedom in this stage of life to free yourself from this important facet of maturity. Find a healthy local church, overlook its flaws, work against your own selfishness and resistance, and become a contributing member. The church needs you, and you need the church.

7.

Find a mentor (or two or seven)

(Becky)

Most of us go through life believing we know what's best for ourselves and don't need anyone to guide us much. And most of us (okay, I was being polite—actually, all of us) are entirely wrong about that. I'm sure you're smart and capable, but even so, the Lord did not create you to walk through life alone. Nor did He make you omniscient. We are all in need of community. And even the smartest among us lack the life experiences of those who have lived longer or within different cultures or environments.

Seeking the wisdom of elders or even peers with different backgrounds and educations can shape our lives and affect our perspectives in ways that we might not learn any other way. Here are just a few dos and don'ts for seeking mentors and making the most of your relationships with them:

Do seek several mentors if you have the opportunity to do so. You can't really have too many. And while it may not be possible to have several who pour into you at the same level of personal involvement, it's always good to have multiple streams of *biblical* wisdom coming your way.

Do honor those you seek to engage by being respectful of their time. You might desire to meet every week, but rather than ask for that specifically, first ask how much time they are comfortable giving you. Once a month might be all they can afford. Keep in mind that many mentor/mentee relationships are kept private, especially if they are working through intense personal sins, accountability issues, or just difficult seasons with others. Don't assume someone has plenty of free time just because you're unaware of how they spend it.

Do show up to your meetings prepared to learn and contribute. This certainly doesn't mean these times together have to be formal or even structured. Often I invite young ladies to sit at the counter in my kitchen while I'm cooking so we can talk (and they can taste-test!) throughout the day. We have no agenda whatsoever, but if our time together is to be helpful, these ladies should show up ready to share and eager to listen. If you just want to glean from interacting with older saints within their everyday life, you will require less prep in advance, just an open heart and mind and readiness for conversation. But if you are involved in some form of struggle and desire specific help, show up prepared to provide the necessary information your mentor will need to be most helpful to you. (For instance, if you read something confusing and want insight, bring the book and mark the passage or write down the specific Scriptures you have questions about.)

Do ask thoughtful questions. It's one of the easiest ways to begin interesting conversations and keep them flowing. If your mentor is married, ask them how they met their spouse. What was the most difficult thing about early married life? How did the Lord redeem that season? What do they like to read? What is their sweetest memory with their parents? What is a piece of unforgettable wisdom they learned from one of their mentors?

The point is to learn about the life of the one you hope to learn from, but not just at a surface level. If you want to know their favorite color, ask that too! But don't stop with those sorts of questions. Find out where the Lord is working in their lives and how you can learn not just from your mentor(s) but from the God who continues to work in their lives.

I recently got to spend time with a precious friend of my oldest daughter. She is one of the best question-askers I've ever met. We were attending a conference together, so we spent a great deal of time sitting quietly side by side, both of us listening to and learning from speakers and teachers much wiser than both of us. But she filled every little coffee break and rest between sessions with the smartest and most thoughtful questions, my favorite of which was, "What's your favorite thing about God right now?" It's been several months since she asked me that, but I still think about it almost every day.

What a great question! The answer changes regularly, but I'm so grateful that because of her, this idea now lingers in my mind. What a beautiful thing to ponder on a daily basis!

Don't replace your Bible with your mentor's words.

Do share your own wisdom. By definition of the relationship, common practice is to seek someone older and wiser to be your mentor. But just because this person might be wiser in general doesn't mean they can't learn from you too. Share your insights when you have them. If you are in a relationship with a good mentor, they will be thrilled to know you are learning and growing, and they will learn from you as well as you spend more time together and discuss important thoughts and ideas.

Don't replace your Bible with your mentor's words. He or she will hopefully be wise and thoughtful, but they will certainly still be an imperfect and sinful human. Glean as much goodness as you can from this person who is hopefully daily striving toward personal holiness, but know that nothing they have to say is as powerful as Scripture. Stay in the Word and let it shape all of your conversations and responses.

Don't gossip. Never *ever* attempt to turn a mentor/mentee meeting into an opportunity to engage in airing every grievance you have against others. If you are experiencing difficult relationships, it makes perfect sense to seek wisdom, but it's important to do so in a way that isn't sinful. Either keep the identity of the difficult person private or seek to get them involved in the conversation. Scripture is very clear about the Lord's views on gossip and slander, and it has nothing good to say about these practices.

Don't be unreliable. Life happens and schedules change, but try to be prompt and reliable to the best of your ability. Even if your mentor assures you that their schedule is flexible, they are making a sacrifice of time and convenience to set aside time for

> We are never too old or wise to learn from others. However, it is important to become a mentor yourself at some point.

you. If you regularly show up late (or not at all), you are wasting the valuable time of your mentor.

Don't be satisfied to be *only* a mentee long-term. To be clear, it is my firm belief that we should all keep mentors in some form throughout our entire lives. We are never too old or wise to learn from others. However, it is important to become a mentor yourself at some point. Look for those around you who might be beginning life experiences similar to those you have recently completed (or at least walked through at some level). Maybe a brand-new student or a young person who is an aunt or uncle for the first time. Maybe a friend in a first serious relationship or someone in a new job or difficult transition.

Whatever the scenario, make yourself available to share your own insights as someone who has been through similar life experiences.

If you will make it a lifelong practice to seek mentors and seek to be a mentor in every phase of life, I am confident you will find your life to be richer, healthier, and more meaningful as you continue to seek the Lord and help others in your life do the same.

8.

Chasing your dreams is overrated

(Jared)

If you asked one hundred young adults what they were preparing to do for a living, I would be willing to bet that the vast majority of them would say something they never even conceived of when they were little kids. I once heard a speaker say that when he was little he wanted to be a sheet metal worker. Why? His dad was a sheet metal worker. He didn't even know what a sheet metal worker was. He just knew that's what his dad did, so that's what he wanted to do when he grew up. Then he grew up, he said, and tried his hand at sheet metal work. Turns out he hated it. Some dreams die more quickly than others!

I have this vague recollection that when I was about three or four I wanted to be a garbage man. Why? Because I would sit on the back steps of my house in Brownsville, Texas, and watch the garbage truck come up the alley to pick up the trash behind my house, and there was a guy hanging off the side of it. I could think of nothing cooler when I was a munchkin than to get to hang off the side of a moving truck. My cousins and I would actually play "garbage men" on our parents' parked cars in the driveway.

But the next thing I wanted to be was an author. In fact, by the first grade, writing books is what I wanted to do when I grew up. I know this, because in my little school progress book, where we pasted our school picture and charted our favorite foods and colors and school subjects, in the space next to "What do you want to be when you grow up?" I wrote *Author*.

I have always wanted to write books. It has been my dream since the first grade. I started writing my first book about halfway through college. It was a novel, and I worked on it in all my spare time. It took me several years to finish. I was so proud of it. In a lot of ways, it was a dream come true. And then I even got an agent for that novel! Somebody "official" liked it and wanted to help get me published. That was a dream come true too!

And then weeks went by. Then months. Then years. I wrote

two more books. None of them were published. I was already neck-deep in local church ministry then, and my dream of being an author was withering. It was a gut check for me.

Have you ever felt like God has gifted and called you to do something, but for some reason He hasn't given you the opportunity or freedom to do it? I have.

I've been able to apply my wrestling with that dream to other areas of my life. It's very easy for a dream or passion to become an object of worship. Maybe for you it's a dream job. Maybe you've got a dream college. Maybe it's an athletic career. Maybe it's just making lots of money. Or perhaps your dream is simply to marry a wonderful spouse and have healthy children.

Then reality hits. Maybe the job prospects aren't as great as you'd expected. Maybe your top school choice rejected your application. Maybe an injury sidelines your athletic opportunities. Maybe your season of singleness is threatening to endure longer than you expected.

Whether it's a dream job or a dream spouse or simply a dream *life*, we are often convinced in our youth that the aim of life is chasing the vision we have for ourselves in our imagination. The world around us is usually no help in this regard! We are told since we're kids to keep dreaming and dream big and never stop chasing our dreams. Then we become adults and realize that advice is largely a load of hot garbage. In a world where everybody is chasing their dreams but very few realize them, we set ourselves and each other up for a grave disappointment.

Idolatry will always do this to us. When we orient ourselves around anything that isn't God, put our whole energies into it and trust it to deliver to us peace and joy and satisfaction—things only God can truly and lastingly give—we will find ourselves miserable and disappointed and, in the worst cases, even depressed and despondent.

Don't let the dream drive you. The apostle James gives a command applicable to this idea when he writes:

> Come now, you who say, "Today or tomorrow we will travel to such and such a city and spend a year there and do business and make a profit." Yet you do not know what tomorrow will bring—what your life will be! For you are like vapor that appears for a little while, then vanishes.
>
> Instead, you should say, "If the Lord wills, we will live and do this or that." But as it is, you boast in your arrogance. (James 4:13–16a)

James is saying that we ought to avoid presumption about how our life is meant to go. This is what happens when we let dreams drive us and give ultimate meaning to our lives. We presume we know how our life is meant to be. We presume that our will is superior to God's will. And the great thing is, many of us do get to achieve these dreams!

For about thirteen years, I tried to get published. Thirteen years! I enjoyed writing so much and believed so strongly I ought to share the gift God has given me with the world that I wouldn't give up. And even though I had begun trying to get published as a novelist, at the end of those thirteen years my first published book was released, and it was a work of nonfiction. My dream for my own life had to change a little bit, but it did come true! And I have to tell you, it was just okay.

I mean, don't get me wrong; it was a blast to find twenty-eight years of dreaming and thirteen years of earnest effort proving true. But having a book published didn't do for my heart what I expected it to, even after all those years of built-up anticipation. My dream coming true made a lousy god. It couldn't do for me what only Christ could do.

> No dream, no matter how audacious, in reality matches the goodness of Christ.

The best job in the world won't be able to do for you what only Christ can do. The best spouse in the world won't be able to meet the deepest needs of your heart like only Christ can. No dream, no matter how audacious, in reality matches the goodness of Christ.

What I learned in those thirteen years, and actually what kept me persevering in my gifts and calling, is realizing that my dream wasn't ultimate. I felt free to continue working hard in this area of my life because I learned to give up the presumption that I had to be published to feel validated, to feel fulfilled, to feel joy. If I hadn't learned to do that, I think I would have given up too early. But because I learned to find my validation, fulfillment, and joy in God alone, I could write without feeling the unbearable pressure of everything riding on it.

I do hope you get to enjoy your dreams coming true. But many of you won't. And that's okay. Dreams are overrated. Shockingly enough, spiritual maturity is so often about watching (and letting) dreams die. And it's okay to be sad when that has to happen. But it's also a joy to realize that the most important things in life—namely Christ and the riches of His grace—cannot be taken from us. Orienting your life around Jesus will, in the end, provide so much more happiness than the pursuit of anything or anyone else.

9.

Take care of
your mind and body

(Becky)

A young, healthy mind and body might be some of the easiest things in life to take for granted *when you are young and healthy.* When everything is working properly and nothing hurts or bends the wrong way or is the wrong color, we tend to feel no urgency to care for all of the moving parts. There will be time for that later, right? The problem is that not only does this idea not hold up practically, but the Bible teaches against living this way.

First Corinthians 6:19–20 reads, "Don't you know that your body is a temple of the Holy Spirit who is in you, whom you have from God? You are not your own, for you were bought at a price. So glorify God with your body." In other words, these bodies don't even belong to us. They are God's, and He has instructed us to care for them. Now, the primary thrust of that passage is not about physical health and fitness, but about abstaining from sexual immorality. But the larger point remains: what we do with our bodies can either glorify God . . . or not.

I'm neither a personal trainer nor a nutritionist, so I'm not here to pretend to be the expert on what you should eat or how you should move your body. Entire industries exist to help guide those decisions. However, if we're going to be good stewards of the gift of our bodies, we each have the responsibility to figure out the best way to do those things. It doesn't mean we should all train like CrossFitters or Olympic athletes or weigh every single bite of food we eat and treat our bodies like science experiments. But it *does* mean that we should avoid laziness, keep our bodies moving, and fuel ourselves with healthy nutrients.

All of our bodies are different and respond to things like food and stress differently, so the command is less about a specific list of things to do and more about understanding our own needs and limits. We must prayerfully consider how to care for ourselves so that we might use our bodies in ways that best honor our Creator. This means good rest, good fuel, and healthy, consistent movement to keep our bodies functioning well to the best of our ability.

And our minds are equally as important as our bodies. More than ever before, we face the potential to clutter our minds with an onslaught of information from thousands of sources in any given moment. Just holding our phones in our hands means we have access to literally unlimited correspondence, entertainment, and information. The social media phenomenon in particular poses a real danger to our ability to have meaningful conversations, to pay attention to more substantive sermons, to read deeper books (like the Bible), and to generally relate to others in "the real world" without awkwardness or anxiety.

> **Have you ever considered that Jesus Christ Himself needed rest?**

Distraction throws itself at us at every turn, and if we aren't careful, our minds can so quickly become filled with everything from trivial information to destructive misinformation, crowding out important and needed truth and Scripture.

Have you ever considered that Jesus Christ Himself needed rest? We read in Luke 5:16 that "he often withdrew to deserted places and prayed." If the Lord of the universe needed this kind of rest for His mind, how could we possibly imagine that we are above it? We must take time to withdraw from busyness, seek moments of quiet where we are free from distraction, and refocus on prayer and communion with the Lord. Again, this can look different for every person, but it can't be neglected if we expect to remain physically and spiritually healthy.

I once had a young man ask me how he can know if he's getting healthy rest or just being lazy. It's an excellent question, especially for those who tend to lean more toward laziness than production. We can easily justify laziness as needing rest, can't we?

> Our bodies and minds are our primary tools for any form of ministry we can hope to carry out in this life, so we must care for them to keep them fit for ministry.

Unfortunately, I don't have a checklist or formula for what is the perfect ratio of activity to rest, nor do I believe everyone should have the same checklist or formula even if a good one did exist. My answer then is what I still believe to be true. The only way to know for sure if you are in the "healthy zone" is through prayer and ongoing communion with the One who created your body. If you worry that you are being lazy, ask the Lord to convict you in this area. If you worry that you're never sitting still or getting enough rest, ask the Lord to convict you of that. He will.

The bottom line is that our bodies and minds are our primary tools for any form of ministry we can hope to carry out in this life, so we must care for them to keep them fit for ministry. You don't need to have a fitness plan that looks anything like anyone else you know, but you do need to steward the body the Lord has given you in healthy ways if you are to remain obedient to whatever calling He has on your life. As much as you can, stay active, fuel your body well, renew your mind, and get some rest. And most of all, keep an ongoing conversation underway with the Lord so that you can ask Him to help guide you in these efforts.

Take care with money

(Jared)

I stink with money. I'm just the worst. Even when I've been able to make good money, I hate thinking about it, managing it, and planning for the future with it. My eyes glaze over looking at spreadsheets or financial accounts. My brain starts to hurt whenever I have to do anything that even smells like accounting. And I've always been this way. I've always had a weird relationship with money.

When I was a young adult, I didn't have a whole lot of it. Becky and I got married when I was twenty, and she brought a lot of needed wisdom and insight to my financial equations. In those early days together, we worked hard for not a whole lot. At one point, we worked five jobs between us just to pay the bills and put me through college. Education cost a lot less then than it does now, but it still wasn't cheap. My parents could not afford to pay for my college education, so we did the best we could. I started out in a local community college, and even after I transferred to a state school, we paid as I went. It took me six years to finish, but when I did, at least we didn't have the massive student loan debts some of my peers had accumulated and would take years to pay off.

One thing I remember from some of my classes is how I was pushed to take my studies a bit more seriously than those who were there on their parents' dime. If I failed a class, I would have to pay by myself to take it again! So I was a more diligent student, knowing I had to pay out of my own pocket for the classes I was taking.

You would've thought that would set me on a great trajectory for sound financial thinking. But I'm an idiot, so it didn't.

I'm more of a spender, and Becky is more of a saver. This dynamic has been the source of not a few conflicts in our life together. Money is such a tricky thing. I still don't like to think about it too much, but I have learned a few things the hard way about its trickiness.

For one, if you grew up in a family that had a lot of money, you might not fully understand the value of it. Or you could have picked up, without even meaning to, a sense of entitlement. Maybe it's given you an outlook on people who don't have much money that is less than gracious. Money can be tricky like that.

If you didn't grow up in a family that had a lot of money, you might actually *over*estimate the value of money. You might be tempted to think that if you just had a certain amount of money, you'd finally be happy or at peace. Money can be tricky like that too.

Jesus warned about money constantly. You might even get the impression that Jesus was declaring money itself evil. But He wasn't. You might have remembered that the Bible says money is the root of all evil. But it isn't. No, this is what the apostle Paul says to his young disciple Timothy: "For the love of money is a root of all kinds of evil, and by craving it, some have wandered away from the faith and pierced themselves with many griefs" (1 Tim. 6:10).

It's the "love of money" that is a root of all kinds of evil. I believe that money is our modern age's number one god, the number one thing that rivals the one true God for our affections. You might think the number one idol is power or fame or sex, but so much of our thinking about those things is tied

> The one who is stingy with his money is in just as much bondage to the idol of it as the one who wastes it.

up in the common denominator of money. It really is an idolatry at the root of all kinds of other idolatries.

And when Jesus is warning about money and the dangers of being rich, He's not saying that money itself or being rich itself is sinful. Rather, He's saying these are incredibly vulnerable positions. Riches don't just buy things; they seem to buy security, authority, and peace.

You have to be very careful in your pursuit of money. Because it's tricky, you could go the wrong way spending too much or holding on to it too much. The one who is stingy with his money is in just as much bondage to the idol of it as the one who wastes it.

Remember that money is a neutral goal. Money is a tool. It's a tool like rope. Like rope, you can either hang yourself with it or pull someone out of a ditch.*

So as you earn, remember to be generous. Remember to support your church and the work of God's mission in the world. This is a way to express gratitude to God for the gift of provision. It's really all His money anyway.

---

* Jared C. Wilson, *The Pastor's Justification: Applying the Work of Christ in Your Life and Ministry* (Wheaton, IL: Crossway, 2013), 53.

Remember to save in such a way that you are prepared for lean seasons or even disastrous circumstances in the future. Remember to save so that you can take care of your family and loved ones for years to come.

And remember in your spending to be thankful, thoughtful, and joyful—not indulgent, careless, and wasteful.

The number of Americans drowning in debt increases exponentially every year, and the retirement age continues to rise as well. We are trained by our culture, and sometimes our families, to spend more than we earn, to put off savings, and to think of money as only for self-enrichment. There's a reason the Bible contains so many warnings about money. The bad habits we develop when we're young can set us up for much heartache later on, especially considering the burden we may place on others because of our lack of financial wisdom.

> Remember in your spending to be thankful, thoughtful, and joyful—not indulgent, careless, and wasteful.

Start now. Be wary of money's trickiness. Seek your identity and validation only in what Christ has done for you in the gospel, so that money will have no hold on you. You might miss out on some earthly treasures, but that stuff shrivels up and dies anyway. Instead, you will be laying up treasures you'll get to enjoy for all eternity (Matt. 6:20).

11.

Never try to be the expert in the room

(Becky)

Never try to be the expert in the room. Instead, always try to be the person who learns the most.

One of the greatest signs of intelligence is a realization that there is always more to learn. And one of my favorite examples of how this works itself out in real life just happens to be my husband, Jared. For years he has been studying, writing, teaching and preaching, and traveling to share his learning and experience with people all over the world and in all different contexts. When he travels, it is usually because someone has hired him to come teach, preach, or coach. By definition of the engagement, he should be the "expert" in the room. They desire to learn from him. But what always stands out to me is that one of the first things he does as soon as we get into a car or sit around a table with our hosts or those in attendance is that he begins to ask questions. If he's at a church, he wants to learn about their history, their staff, their people. What is the culture like? How long has the pastor been there? What are the biggest challenges they're currently facing? How well do they know other churches in the area, and do they have good relationships with them? If it's a school, he asks about the leadership, the degree programs, the most influential professors, etc.

> One of the greatest signs of intelligence is a realization that there is always more to learn.

Even though he is the one who has been brought in to teach or preach or coach, he understands that while his knowledge and wisdom are valuable, they are much more helpful if he is able to apply them effectively to the specific listeners he is addressing.

For several years in a row, we traveled to Australia, where Jared was able to teach and preach in various churches and conferences throughout Tasmania and Sydney and a few other areas mostly along the eastern coast of the country. I'm sure it isn't difficult to imagine that there are some pretty distinct differences between America and Australia, but even the cultures of Sydney and Tasmania are almost complete opposites. Sydney is the largest, most highly populated city in Australia, and Tasmania is one of the most rural, sparsely populated places I've ever visited. The lifestyles have little to nothing in common, so needless to say, it's important to understand how ministry opportunities might differ depending on those contexts. Each time we have visited, Jared has learned a bit more about the lifestyles, ministry challenges, and cultural hot topics specific to each location so that he can better understand how to minister to the people under his teaching.

Unlike my husband, I'm pretty sure I should never ever teach much of anything to anybody ever in any kind of formal setting. I do not have the gift of teaching, and I take the book of James way too seriously to pretend like I do.* But I'm a mom, so there are at least two people I've been entrusted to teach and lead throughout their entire lives—my daughters. I've tried to teach them everything from how to tie their shoes and brush their teeth to how to cling to Christ and represent the gospel well over the years.

---

* "Not many should become teachers, my brothers, because you know that we will receive a stricter judgment" (James 3:1).

One of the things I've taken great joy in teaching them is how to cook and host and keep a welcoming home. Hospitality is probably my strongest area of giftedness, and I have had lots of practice, so I enjoy passing along some of my knowledge and experience in that area. (More on that in chapter 13.) But my oldest daughter recently discovered that she suffers from a rare autoimmune disease that has required her to adjust her diet fairly significantly. She tries to strictly follow an anti-inflammatory diet, which means no gluten, no dairy, and no processed sugar, and even limitations on things that are usually considered healthy like nightshade vegetables. So now, even though I have twice as many years of experience cooking as she does, I am learning from her about more specialized recipes and tasty ingredients that fit within her eating plan.

Based on our ages alone and the number of dishes we have each cooked throughout our lives, most people would agree that she should be the one continually learning from me. And she does. But that doesn't mean I can't learn plenty from her too. She has done far more research and cooked and tasted far more gluten-free, dairy-free, sugar-free meals than I have, so I am grateful to learn from her experience and let her help me better serve my guests with similar dietary restrictions.

Of course, these are just personal examples from my own

life, but the same idea is applicable in almost any situation involving an exchange of ideas with other people. You can be far better educated than everyone else in the room and even be a well-studied "expert" on the main topic of conversation, but you can never know better than someone else their own life experience, background, or their ideas about any given subject. The solution to this is so simple: Ask questions. Learn.

12.

Find your friends carefully

(Jared)

When I was a senior in high school, my parents went out of town and left my younger brother and me home alone for a few days. They'd gone on overnight trips before, but this was the first extended absence they'd trusted us with. Very close to their worst nightmare came true.

On the Sunday evening of their trip, I was driving my brother and a friend after youth group to Blockbuster to rent a movie, and on a busy street just outside my own neighborhood, a car turned left against the traffic right in front of me. I smashed into them going almost fifty miles an hour.

It was a significant crash. Both of our vehicles were totaled. But thankfully nobody was seriously hurt. My brother in the back seat of the family station wagon had some serious bruising from the seatbelt across his waist, but while my buddy and I were a little shaken up, we were physically unscathed.

The driver of the other car had obviously been drinking. You could smell the alcohol coming out of his vehicle, when he and his many friends spilled out of it like clowns emerging from a circus car. They were all about my age. In fact, we were high school classmates. The police officer who responded to the scene spent a lot of time with them, though I don't recall if he took them into custody or ticketed them.

Here's what I remember most: as my two passengers and I stood there sorting through the shock of everything, there was a steady stream of friends from youth group who, having to pass the accident on their ways home, stopped and got out to check on us and support us. The older couple who lived across the street from me somehow became aware of the accident and came out to the main road. The husband knew my parents were away, so he was making sure we were okay. And later, when he called my dad, he said, "Jared and Jeremy are okay. And I have to tell you, I was really impressed by the quality of their friends."

I've never forgotten that. My neighbor had some negative things to say about the other driver's friends! But as he made a comparison, he was encouraged to see that the teenage boys who'd stopped to check on us were thoughtful, kind, and respectful. They offered to pray for us, offered to give us a ride, to go call someone. This was all a reminder to me that it really, really matters what kinds of friends you have.

> **The friends you have don't just keep you entertained. They shape your life. They affect your moods. They can alter your direction in life.**

The friends you have don't just keep you entertained. They shape your life. They affect your moods. They can alter your direction in life.

The Bible speaks to this concept at numerous points. For instance, the book of Proverbs contains lots of spiritual counsel related to friendship. We're told not to be friends with hot-tempered people (22:24). We're told that a friend's sweetness is better than being alone (27:9). We're even told to be careful about having too many superficial friends (18:24). In 1 Corinthians 15:33, Paul gives this explicit warning: "Do not be deceived: 'Bad company corrupts good morals.'"

Here's the reality: who you commit your life to will shape

you, for good or bad. Our relational communities are so important for our own sense of identity, meaning, and even security.

This is important especially if you're planning to leave home and, in effect, start a new life in a new town or at a new school. The need for belonging is so strong within us that very often we will settle for it in the first or easiest places of welcome. And many times we'll overlook red flags about those places of belonging. So we must be on guard. We must choose our friends wisely. We should not embrace belonging or define our identity in communities that reject biblical teaching or otherwise lead us to rebel against God.

I am convinced that many young people who have begun identifying as gay or transgender are doing so out of a deep hurt and a deep sense of unbelonging. Then these communities come along to welcome and promise a home, a place of understanding, and a defining of oneself that seems hard to find elsewhere.

This dynamic can take place with any believer who longs for identity and community and who isn't firmly rooted in the gospel and a community of faith centered on that gospel. It may not be sexual or gender confusion that leads you to drift away. It may just be a group that has no esteem for God's Word, for objective morality, for righteous living, and the like. Those kinds of friends may be good for a laugh or a lift, but when crises of faith come, when the bottom falls out from under you, they will be unable to speak life-giving words of eternal truth to encourage and help you. Or worse, if you spend enough time with them, you may not even care that they can't.

If you choose your friends wisely, however, you'll have brothers and sisters who walk with you continually through the worst moments of your life and help you grow old gracefully.

13.

Practice hospitality

(Becky)

I suspect that when many of you hear the word *hospitality*, you assume it's something that doesn't apply much to your life yet. Maybe it's something you'll practice when you get older, get more "settled," and have a home of your own, a place where you can invite people to dinner or have them over for game or movie nights. But people at every stage of life are not only capable of practicing hospitality, but commanded by Scripture to do so.

Maybe we should start by defining the word.

Hospitality, very simply, is "the friendly reception and treatment of guests or strangers."* Or, to expound a bit more, hospitality is "the quality or disposition of receiving and treating guests and strangers in a warm, friendly, generous way."†

Notice what this definition doesn't say. It says nothing about age. Nothing about needing a house or apartment. Nothing about spending money or having lots of material things to offer. Hospitality—in its truest, most meaningful form—is a condition of the heart. So it follows that if you have a heart, you have the ability to practice hospitality.

> Hospitality is the quality or disposition of receiving and treating guests and strangers in a warm, friendly, generous way.

And to emphasize the point even further, if your heart is *not* the source of the hospitality, whatever actions you produce will likely not seem very hospitable to the recipient. The disposition and attitude of our hearts must drive our actions. Otherwise, our actions may not feel like hospitality at all.

Why is this so important? Honestly, this could be its own book

---

* Dictionary.com, s.v. "hospitality," https://www.dictionary.com/browse/hospitality.
† Dictionary.com, s.v. "hospitality."

(and many have been written on this subject), but for the sake of brevity, I'll just list three:

1. HOSPITALITY CREATES COMMUNITY LIKE VERY FEW THINGS CAN.

I am a firm believer that we all need each other. I am also a firm believer that we cultivate relationships best when we invite people into our personal lives, whether that be having them over for dinner, taking walks together, or even just riding together to other events and talking during the drive. There is something that happens in those more private moments that just can't be duplicated in public settings like schools or restaurants or sometimes even churches. It can feel pretty lonely in this world when sin becomes more and more prominent, and it seems like you are the only person who still believes in purity or truth or caring for the least of these. Or when you are in the middle of a particularly difficult struggle, and you feel like no one understands. The Bible boldly promises us that none of these things will go away before heaven.

Trouble and suffering will come to each of us in some form or fashion, but when it does, what a wonderful and needed blessing to have friends far and wide who can support us through prayer or any number of other ways just because we met together in someone's living room a few years ago and began a friendship. It's one of my favorite things of all time to know that I have been instrumental in bringing people together who might not have ever met otherwise, just because they shared a meal in my home and now keep in touch in other ways. And we can all affect people in this way. We can all build relationships and then connect them to each other.

2. WE ARE ALL EQUIPPED AND QUALIFIED TO PRACTICE HOSPITALITY.

Hospitality requires no special skills at all. We've already established that if you have a heart, you have the ability to practice hospitality. And if you make a habit of it, it can have a big impact in pointing people to Christ. Hospitality is not a lesser gift. It can actually be life-changing.

> If you have a heart, you have the ability to practice hospitality.

Consider the testimony of Rosaria Butterfield. She was a feminist, activist, lesbian professor who was invited into the homes of some Christian friends. Initially, she only agreed so that she could ridicule them and argue against everything they stood for. But after about two years of joining them in their home and experiencing their welcome and care for her, she eventually came to know the Lord. She would tell you that it wasn't a bunch of casseroles that changed her life, but she would just as quickly tell you that the sharing of those casseroles is what put her in the time and place and right frame of mind to receive the Holy Spirit and surrender to Christ.

3. THERE ARE NO REAL RULES TO HOSPITALITY!

So I already said we can all do this, but now I want you to know that we can all do it in completely different ways, and it's totally fine! Remember that what we're after here is kindness and generosity. A sense of welcome. For me, that looks most often like having people over for dinner or bringing them a meal. For you, it might be inviting them to meet you for coffee. Or sending them an encouraging note. It could mean talking about favorite books or movies or music together. Or it could be as simple as noticing someone who looks like they could use a friend and just saying hello and offering a warm smile and a genuine "How are you?" followed by an attentive ear.

Where can we practice these things? Let's start with our church.

It is the responsibility of every believer to make sure their church is a welcoming, friendly, loving place for guests and for each other. We should extend the love of Christ to every person we encounter every chance we get. There are many ways to do that. Hold doors. Smile. Help with young children when appropriate. Sign up for one of the service teams. Pray for each other! Find out needs that you can meet during the week. Check in with people you haven't seen in a while. Write notes. Sometimes you can't imagine what just a few words can do to encourage people.

What about your school? Do you respect your professors and other school personnel and try to make their jobs easier by being a good student and respectful resident? Do you greet your friends warmly, kindly, and joyfully? Do you set an example for others by the way you conduct yourself?

> No matter where we are, there are always opportunities to show hospitality to those around us.

How does this look at home? Well, how do you treat your parents, siblings, or roommates? What about when there are guests in your home even if you didn't invite them? Do you contribute to a loving atmosphere if your parents or roommates have guests? Are you kind to other people's children in your home even if they are younger than you and maybe a little annoying?

No matter where we are, there are always opportunities to show hospitality to those around us. We all have the capability to be kind and friendly. And even if we don't have money or material things to give, we can all be generous in other ways with things like time, service, encouragement, and prayers, just to name a few.

But why does this really matter? Why can't we just keep to ourselves and mind our own business? Isn't it good enough if I just don't bother anybody?

Well, no. It isn't. And I'll give you three reasons why this is so important and not at all optional.

1. THE BIBLE COMMANDS IT.

Romans 12:13, Galatians 6:10, Hebrews 13:2 and 13:16, and 1 Peter 4:9 are just a few of the places where we're exhorted to hospitality. And there are more. Scripture commands that we be hospitable. To be obedient believers, we all need to find ways to practice hospitality even if it looks very different for each of us.

2. WE ALL DESPERATELY NEED IT FROM EACH OTHER.

Consider Paul's words to Timothy in 2 Timothy 1:16: "May the Lord grant mercy to the household of Onesiphorus, because he often refreshed me and was not ashamed of my chains." This is just one of many biblical examples, but I bet we could all think of present-day examples, either for ourselves or people we know and love. Sometimes we are just struggling and need a safe place to rest. Probably not at the level that Paul needed! Nevertheless, we all need each other's hospitality to help us through difficult times. We need the encouragement found in the company of fellow believers who will walk with us and help us carry our burdens. We need places to feel welcome even as the world around us becomes more and more unwelcome for Christians. And we need refreshment to get back out there and continue the fight.

Finally:

3. IT CREATES OPPORTUNITIES TO SHARE THE GOSPEL.

Think about all the relationships with those you regularly encounter, everyone from your closest friends and family members to the person on campus that you've only made accidental eye contact with once and never spoken to. Which ones are most likely to listen to you when you share your heart for Christ? Or to even notice that there's something different about you that they might want to know about? Now consider this: If you were to identify just one person on the far end of that spectrum, how might you go about showing them hospitality so that it might eventually lead to the gospel? Maybe it's just initially asking them how they're doing and then checking in with them regularly. You don't have to whack them over the head with your Bible the very first time you talk to them (or ever). You don't even have to quote Scripture to them right away. Just start with kindness. Consider that definition of hospitality again: *the quality or disposition of receiving and treating guests and strangers in a warm, friendly, generous way.*

Start there. Warm. Friendly. Generous. Maybe that will lead to "I'll pray for you" during a difficult time. Or, "Hey, you should come to church with me sometime!" And just maybe it will one day lead to an entire life changed through a little hospitality. The Bible itself tells us in Romans 2:4 that it is God's kindness that leads us to repentance. How fitting then that He might allow us to play a role in His bringing people to Himself through our own kindness, through our reflection of Him. This is one of the ways we represent the gospel well.

But now for maybe the biggest question of all—*how* do we do this? How do we get up every single day and somehow decide that we will be kind, warm, encouraging, and hospitable even if there's no coffee?

I'm sure that many of us feel quite the opposite some days. We're tired. We're stressed. We're busy. Some of us are lonely. Maybe afraid. This world is not becoming easier to live in. And sometimes it's difficult enough to pick ourselves up out of bed in the morning without worrying about trying to think of ways to serve everyone else. How in the world do we find the strength to do this?

The bad news? I don't think we can. At least, not within our own power. But here's the good news: if we are in Christ, we have a Helper. The Holy Spirit empowers us through His presence to become more like Christ as we walk with Him and allow Him to change us—not through our efforts, but through the power of the gospel.

14.

Marriage won't complete you

(Jared)

When I was a kid, I either always had a girlfriend or always *wanted* a girlfriend. And then Becky and I started dating when I was seventeen and got married when I was twenty. In my mind, this was the way life was supposed to go. I had no conception of my life as being lived as a single person.

Whether you have a significant other at this point or not, you may be thinking the same thing. We envision the steps of growing up and into mature adulthood as always entailing moving out, getting a job, and getting married. But for an increasing number of American singles, that does not appear to be in the picture. In fact, in the past few years, our country hit an all-time low in marriage rates.* And evangelicalism has not been immune to this phenomenon. More and more people are putting off marriage till they're older or forgoing marriage altogether.

If you're a Christian who's grown up in an evangelical church, you may be tempted to think this is the worst thing that could ever happen to you. I imagine I would've thought so too. A lot of us grow up in cultures where marriage and parenting aren't just celebrated and honored but almost held as non-negotiables for adult faithfulness. Many single friends I've talked to over the last few years have shared how they often feel like second-class citizens in their churches—especially as they get older and still remain single.

> In 1 Corinthians 7:32–38, Paul positions singleness as an *advantage* over marriage, because it frees a Christian to think in more intense ways about pursuing the kingdom of God.

There is one thing we must get a lot better at doing: simultaneously holding up marriage as a wonderful

---

* Gaby Galvin, "U.S. Marriage Rate Hits Historic Low," US News & World Report, April 29, 2020, https://www.usnews.com/news/healthiest-communities/articles/2020-04-29/us-marriage-rate-drops-to-record-low.

gift and worthy aspiration (Heb. 13:4) while remembering that one's marital status doesn't make one a better Christian. In fact, in 1 Corinthians 7:32–38, Paul positions singleness as an *advantage* over marriage, because it frees a Christian to think in more intense ways about pursuing the kingdom of God. So if you're single—and end up being single for a while—I want to say to you that desiring marriage is a good thing, but there is no spouse that will fix you, complete you, or heal you like only Jesus can. You may be thinking of marriage as the antidote to all your longing and struggle, but it isn't.

Similarly, if you're married or plan soon to be, I want to tell you the same thing! You should work hard not to expect from your spouse the kind of fulfillment only Christ can give you. For one thing, every sinner is married to another sinner. We are all broken, flawed, and beset with indwelling sin. So looking for perfection from those unable to be perfect is a losing game. And for another thing, we are all finite persons. We have limited capacities, limited resources. We all need filling up. What happens in a marriage when both parties are looking to the other to constantly be pouring out? A whole lot of tension and frustration.

Yes, the Bible says that a man and woman joined together in marriage are "one flesh" (Gen. 2:24; Matt. 19:6), but this does not make a single person "half a flesh" any more than it makes one member of the Trinity 33.3 percent God! Nor does it mean that married couples will find perfect satisfaction in each other. No, that can only come from the Lord.

Your spouse won't satisfy the deepest needs of your heart. Thinking so only sets you—and them—up for heartache, as only Christ can fulfill you completely. Look to Jesus for your satisfaction and fulfillment, and you will find that, whether single or married, your life will be joyfully bearable and an increasing delight.

15.

Go outside

(Becky)

We can certainly learn plenty from computer screens (and technology of every kind), but—for the sake of your soul—go outside! Go outside and look around as often as you can. For so many reasons, your mind and body need the outdoors. I'll cover just two reasons here.

1. THE GLORY OF GOD IS DECLARED BY THE NATURAL WORLD.

Have you ever considered how many exquisite sensory experiences live just outside your windows? Nature presents a brilliant masterpiece of art, science, theology, and more. The vibrant colors displayed through flowers and butterflies. Bird-song lingering in the breeze. The delight of warm, healthy grass under your bare feet. Fresh air filling your lungs with just a hint of honeysuckle fragrance. And that adorable little squirrel who keeps coming right up onto your deck to see if you left him any nuts today. (I always do. Also, can you tell spring is just beginning as I write this?) Do you ever take "little things" like these for granted? We all do. Every day.

But consider this: none of these things are accidents. They are gifts crafted by the Father Himself for our enjoyment. Think about it. Beauty and pleasure contribute little if anything to functionality. Flowers could serve the same purpose if they were all the same size, shape, and color. For that matter, color is basically worthless. We don't need it to survive. Clean air with no fragrance serves our lungs every bit as well as a breeze carrying the scent of freshly cut grass and the neighbor's lavender bushes. But God delights in our enjoyment of His creation. It's part of His conversation with us. He says "I want your soul to be refreshed" every time we inhale sweetly perfumed air. He says "I want you to be filled with joy and wonder" every time we watch a baby bird stumble and then take flight for the first time. He says "I want you to remember Me" every time we study His handiwork in the artistry of a canna leaf or the perfect symmetry of a fern. He says "I like to hear you laugh" when we witness two squirrels chasing each other and fighting over the same nut even though there's an untouched pile a few feet away.

Every sunrise reminds us of new mercies. Every rainfall tells a story of His provision. Every rainbow speaks a promise.

Psalm 19:1 tells us that "the heavens declare the glory of God, and the expanse proclaims the work of his hands." Theologians call the perception we can have of God from the created world "general revelation," and obviously we need the "special revelation" of the Scriptures (and Christ's gospel in them) to be reconciled to our Creator, but we can still behold some of the glorious wonders of our Creator through the wonderful world He has created.

> Every sunrise reminds us of new mercies. Every rainfall tells a story of His provision. Every rainbow speaks a promise.

I admit that I can be rather ridiculous in my enjoyment of nature. My daughters have rolled their eyes at me many times when I squeal with delight at the sight of some little bird or ladybug or lizard. Imagine my reaction to watching *baby sea turtles* find their way into the ocean a few years ago. Forget about it. I might have (definitely) cried.

I am not suggesting that we all have to enjoy the outdoors in the same ways or even in the same amounts. But many times I have found myself alone in nature and realized that I was the only witness to something glorious happening right before my eyes, that the Lord saw fit to put His artistry and power on display just for me. I believe He desires to do that for each of us, and it's a conversation we do not want to miss. Make time for these conversations. Experience what He called "good" during creation and desires to share with you now. Take joy in what He has made for His glory and your enjoyment. It will serve your mind and body in immeasurable ways.

2. THE OUTSIDE WORLD CAN HELP YOU BATTLE SIN.

Of course, sin can happen outside just as easily and often as it does inside. Unfortunately, being present in the beauty of nature doesn't magically remove the ugliness of our sin nature. However, I could reasonably argue that it's much more difficult to hide in our sin when we are outside in wide open spaces. Further, it is easier to forget our sinful desires when a majestic moment in nature takes our breath away and changes the subject of our thoughts.

In a sermon many years ago, John Piper pointed out the absence of windows in stores that sell pornography.* He observed

---

* John Piper, "Do You See the Joy of God in the Sun? Part 2," sermon preached at Bethlehem Baptist Church, August 26, 1990, Desiring God, https://www.desiringgod.org/messages/do-you-see-the-joy-of-god-in-the-sun-part-2.

that the reason for this is that it is very difficult to engage in this particular sin when we look at the sky. I couldn't agree more, but I also think the same idea would apply to most any sin. Fully engaging in the grandeur of nature reminds us of our smallness and makes us forgetful of our small desires. When we consider God's work during creation, we must remember that we were specifically designed to enjoy it!

Things changed dramatically when sin entered the world, but not so much that this desire was completely removed from us. Consider Barnabas Piper's words:

> The world God created was not ok or decent or fine; it was exactly right. It was good. . . .
>
> But what we often forget is that sin and the curse did not evaporate the good and replace it. They did not recreate the world as a heinously evil hellscape. Sin corrupted the good, but the world still has God's fingerprints all over it and tendrils of Eden woven through it. Nothing is completely as it should be, but neither is the world utterly corrupt. The good that once defined all of creation still shines throughout it.[*]

[*] Barnabas Piper, *Hoping for Happiness: Turning Life's Most Elusive Feeling into Lasting Reality* (Epsom, UK: The Good Book Company, 2020), 69.

We were created for Eden, and we still have desires for Eden. We belong in nature. Today it isn't as perfect as it once was or will be when Christ returns, but we are much closer to it when we spend time outside than when we surround ourselves with closed doors and windows or stare at screens too long. Even if only for a few brief moments, develop a daily habit of walking away from whatever is demanding too much of your attention (especially if it is sinful) to go look at the sky. Your future self will thank you.

16.

Learn to be friends with Jesus

(Jared)

I'm sure you've heard it said that "Christianity isn't a religion; it's a relationship." But what does that mean (beyond the clichéd slogan, at least)?

A lot of Christian young people grow up relating to Jesus more as an *idea* and less as a *person*. This dysfunction stems from a form of religion that is self-focused and performance-based. Here's how it usually works: We spend a lot of years treating the Bible as a book of inspirational quotes and moralistic advice. We spend a lot of years treating the "pure religion" (James 1:27) of

Christianity as a vast self-improvement project. And thus we end up treating Jesus like a sidekick or guru.

Jesus is *not* a sidekick or guru. He is the center of the universe, or He is nothing.

And if we do not take care that our Christianity is rooted in real relationship with Jesus, we will be very vulnerable to all kinds of distortions of our faith. We may compromise biblical doctrine because it doesn't suit our personal tastes. We may compromise righteous living because it doesn't suit our personal convenience. And errors like these aren't just the fruit of disordered thinking; they are the fruit of a disordered heart. The heart that has self on the throne instead of Jesus cannot stand strong against temptation of any kind.

> Don't assume that just because you agree to certain doctrinal truths or just because you've spent all your life in a church setting that your intimacy with Him is genuine.

As you prepare to make the faith your own, to discover what it's like navigating the world with your own spirituality leading the way, don't forget to invest in your relationship with Jesus. Don't assume that just because you agree to certain doctrinal truths or just because you've spent all your life in a church setting that your intimacy with Him is genuine.

Further, don't assume that just because you're committed to good works or even serving in a church that your relationship with Jesus is real! One of the scariest passages in all of Scripture, to me, is found in Matthew 7:22–23, where Jesus Himself says:

"On that day many will say to me, 'Lord, Lord, didn't we prophesy in your name, drive out demons in your name, and do many miracles in your name?' Then I will announce to them, 'I never knew you. Depart from me . . .'"

We do not want to be those who get to the day of judgment and plead all of our religiosity before God as verification of our faith. Many people will say, "Jesus, didn't I go to church in Your name? Didn't I serve the poor in Your name? Didn't I set a good example in the youth group in Your name? Didn't I study theology in Your name? Didn't I become a ministry leader in Your name?" And Jesus will say to them, "I have no idea who you are."

Like I said: Scary, isn't it?

Never confuse doing things *for* God with actually being known *by* God.

And the beautiful truth is that, through the gospel, we don't have to wonder if we're friends with Jesus. He has declared His followers friends (John 15:15). We're not employees. We're not even acquaintances. We're friends!

> Never confuse doing things *for* God with actually being known *by* God.

More than that, though, we are also called Jesus' brothers and sisters! And Hebrews 2:11 says Jesus is not ashamed to call us that. Given how sinful we are, He ought to be. But He isn't.

If you're worried that friendship with Jesus entails burdens you can't bear and responsibilities you can't manage, you should know that He's the kind of friend who gives rest to the weary and comfort to the overwhelmed. He's the kind of friend who knows that we will buckle under the weight of religiosity and comes to encourage and support us with His grace. He is gentle. He is warm. He is a fountain of constant and steadfast love.

And He is forgiving. And patient. Jesus never checks His phone when you talk to Him. He never looks over your shoulder for someone more important. He never sighs or sulks about you. And He'll never "tsk tsk" you. He always lives to intercede for you (Heb. 7:25). He'll never turn His back on you (Deut. 31:6).

Jesus understands our weaknesses and temptations (Heb. 4:15); He sympathizes with us. And Jesus will establish you, strengthen you, and guide you. You're not too high-maintenance for Him. You're not too weird or awkward for Him. And we know, because of the cross, that you are not even too sinful for Him.

If you ever are tempted to doubt God's love for you and Christ's commitment to you, look to the cross. It is undeniable and irrefutable proof that Jesus loves us. He could not have paid a higher price or demonstrated a greater love.

Do you see now that Jesus is the best kind of friend you could have? As you're figuring out what kind of company you're going to keep in the months and years ahead, don't forget to invest in your friendship with the one who is an everlasting friend to sinners.

Make a regular part of your day to engage in conversation with Him through the divine dialogue of Scripture reading and prayer. I call these essential spiritual disciplines the divine dialogue because when we study Scripture, God speaks to us, and when we pray, we speak to God. Practicing the dialogue every day—and frequently throughout the day—is the best and primary way to commune with Jesus.

Remember that He's a real person! He's not some corny painting on the wall. He's not a mascot. You may not be able to see Him (yet!), but He can be seen. Risen from the grave bodily and gloriously, He ascended to heaven and is seated at the right hand of the Father. One day we will look into His eyes. One day we will be able to hold His hand and hug His neck. But until that day, we can keep the eyes of our heart focused on Him. Because He's real, and He really loves us.

If you want your Christian faith to endure through all the trials and tribulations of life ahead, you must make sure to be friends with Jesus.

17.

Appreciate people more than you need them

(Becky)

We all need each other. Desperately. The Lord did not design humans to thrive in isolation. We are generally much stronger, healthier, smarter, and more successful when we function within a community of people with the same values working toward the same goal. The Bible itself teaches us this in Romans 12, 1 Corinthians 12, and many other places. But our understanding of that need and how we respond to it is critical to maintaining healthy relationships.

It is good and right to need friends, especially fellow believers with whom we can share important life experiences. The key word, though, is "share." This doesn't necessarily mean equal participation, and it certainly doesn't mean participating in the same ways.

One person who comes to mind immediately as I'm thinking through this is a friend of ours named Ed, who suffers from cerebral palsy. Ed is confined to a wheelchair, which means he will never be able to help his friends with things like moving or major home repairs or childcare or a long list of other activities. And not only can he not be helpful in those ways, but he also has to depend on his friends quite significantly for things like transportation, navigating through certain buildings, etc. In so many categories of life, the scales within his relationships will never be balanced.

Ed needs others in physical ways much more than most of us do. But what he also does is honor and encourage his friends better than just about anyone I've ever met. He understands what the Bible teaches about each of us contributing to the body in the unique ways we're gifted. He obeys Romans 12:3–8 by exercising his gifts of teaching, exhortation, and more. He helps in the ways that he can even as he depends in the ways that he must. And to some, it may look like he receives more help than he is able to offer.

But I disagree. Because if we continue to read in Romans 12, we find in verse 10 the commands to "love one another deeply as brothers and sisters" and "take the lead in honoring one another." And Ed excels at Romans 12:10. He certainly needs people, and likely always will at some level, but he does not take them for granted, and he does not treat people as though he is entitled to their help. He loves. He honors. He values. He appreciates. Without that response, needs quickly lead to entitlement, which is basically just another word for pride.

Now let's apply this idea to marriage. Not all of you reading this book may desire marriage, but this principle is too important to neglect for those who do hope to marry. Contrary to what we find on the silver screens, grooved vinyl, and printed pages of romantic movies, records, and novels, we do not need to be "completed" by another human being. (See chapter 14.) The Lord created us in His own image, whole and thoroughly designed. None of us is a fraction of a person until we find our "other half." However, certainly there are needs that a spouse can and should meet once vows are exchanged. It would be silly to expect

> Just because we want something doesn't mean we need it, and just because we need something doesn't mean our spouse is responsible for providing it.

otherwise. But problems arise when couples begin to label every want as a need or expect each other to meet every need all the time in the exact way they'd like it to be met.

The way to combat both of these errors is with appreciation. First, be thankful to God for the spouse He gave you and then be thankful to your spouse for the ways he or she loves you, helps you, and meets many of your needs. Rather than build a long list in your mind of all the things you wish your spouse would do differently, often convincing yourself that you deserve these things, practice gratitude for the ways they do meet your needs. It is surprising and heartbreaking how quickly a lack of appreciation can lead to an unhealthy view of your spouse, a sense of entitlement, or even destructive behavior like viewing pornography or other inappropriate behavior. We must actively protect our marriages against these things by developing a culture of honor and appreciation for each other and understanding that just because we want something doesn't mean we need it, and just because we need something doesn't mean our spouse is responsible for providing it.

For most of us, seasons of need will ebb and flow. We will go through times of struggle and even suffering throughout our lives and need family and friends to step in and care for us. Sometimes physically in times of illness or financial need.

Sometimes emotionally in times of grief or anxiety. Sometimes spiritually in times of doubt or besetting sin. We should all look to our trusted friends for help in times of any kind of need. But if we need people without appreciating them, this quickly and easily leads to using them and maybe even turning them into idols. See the people who love you as gifts. Appreciate their presence in your life and communicate that to them regularly.

18.

Center on the gospel

(Jared)

As a professor at a Christian seminary and Bible college, I direct all my teaching for all my classes through the paradigm of gospel centrality. And what I've discovered over the years is that while a lot of students have heard the phrasing "gospel centrality" or "gospel-centered," very few can define what the phrasing means. The idea has become more of a slogan or tribal identifier. If you're "gospel-centered," you read certain books, admire certain preachers, go to certain conferences, and scroll certain websites. But somehow, even after engaging in all this "gospely" stuff, very few come away being able to articulate the substance of gospel centrality.

What does it mean?

I want to give you three core principles here that will help you not just make sense of your Christian faith, evaluate the variety of church options available to you, and get more out of your Bible studies, but also that will change your life. The idea of gospel centrality didn't just give me a new ministry philosophy once upon a time; it gave me hope and joy and energy I needed to carry on despite incredible suffering. Here's the first principle of gospel centrality:

1. THE WHOLE BIBLE IS ABOUT JESUS.

Christ is the whole point of all the Scriptures. From Old Testament to New Testament, the entirety of those sixty-six books culminates in and declares the centrality of the Son of God. You may have noticed, of course, that Jesus doesn't appear in the Old Testament. Except, He does! According to His own testimony (John 5:39; Luke 24:27), the Old Testament is all about Him. The preaching of the apostles in the New Testament is all summarized by Christ-centered proclamations of Old Testament texts. And the book of Hebrews gives us a deeper glimpse into the ways the Old Testament is fulfilled and oriented around Jesus Christ.

If we want to have a vibrant faith that is distinctly Christian, we cannot treat the Bible as merely an instruction manual for better behavior, an inspirational storybook for better courage, or a theological reference text for better intellect. The Bible's commands are good. Its inspiration is unparalleled. And its theology is perfect. But the Bible is ultimately and centrally about Jesus. So we have to read, study, teach, and preach the Bible as if He is the point.

2. PEOPLE REALLY CHANGE BY GRACE, NOT LAW.

Most of us have a law-centered approach to personal change. We think we know how to effect change in people—we tell them to change! And if that doesn't work, we repeat the command and perhaps turn up the volume. We tell them more and more loudly. Maybe we hold out rewards for their change. Or threats if they don't change. We give them practical application, showing them *how* to implement change.

But the best this approach can achieve is behavior modification. And

> Christianity is about real transformation, from the inside out. We're not just interested in better behavior but a new heart.

behavior modification is good if all you care about is efficiency and comfort. Christianity, however, is about real transformation, from the inside out. We're not just interested in better behavior but a new heart.

> Somehow, knowing that in Christ the work is finished actually empowers us to get to work!

What we learn over and over again in the Bible is that one cannot get a new heart through obedience to commandments. The law of God is good, but it cannot change people the way only the gospel can. In fact, the only thing the New Testament identifies as transforming power is the Holy Spirit working through the message of the gospel.

In Titus 2:11–12 (ESV), Paul says that grace is "training" us to renounce unrighteousness and live godly lives. Somehow, knowing that in Christ the work is finished actually empowers us to get to work! And in 2 Corinthians 3:18, Paul says that it is by beholding Christ that we are transformed into Christlikeness. Somehow, seeing Christ is the way to become more like Him.

People change—the way Christianity counts change—by the power of grace through the glory of Jesus.

3. OUR ULTIMATE VALIDATION MUST COME FROM THE GOSPEL.

At its heart, the gospel—the good news that Jesus has died on the cross to forgive sinners and was raised from the dead to conquer death for them and purchase their eternal life—is announcing that a sinner's justification comes by faith alone in Christ alone. But we need to get much better at pushing that justification, so to speak, into every corner of the room.

What I mean is this: most of us understand that there is a point of conversion for us where we are said to "get saved." You prayed a prayer, walked an aisle, spoke to a friend or family member or pastor, and at some point in that process, you passed from darkness to light and from death to life. But too many of us assume this is the final stop in the gospel's work in our life. We believe that the gospel is for lost people, and once you're found, you don't really need it any more. This is not the way the Bible speaks about the gospel.

> Our ultimate validation every single day of our life—and on the last day of our life—must come not from what we have done but from what Jesus has done on our behalf.

In 1 Corinthians 15:1–2, Paul tells us that the gospel isn't just something we "received" (past tense); it's also something that we "stand" on (present tense) and are "being saved" by (present-future tense). Clearly the gospel is power beyond our conversion experience!

Yes, in fact, the gospel speaks to our whole Christian life. We are not saved by the gospel into a world of merit by performance. We don't maintain our status as saved people through our works. And our assurance and spiritual security cannot come through our own spirituality. All of this must come from what Christ has done for us. Our ultimate validation every single day of our life—and on the last day of our life—must come not from what we have done but from what Jesus has done on our behalf. Our hope always is Jesus. Our validation always is from the gospel.

You know, most of us experience in life a natural drift toward a kind of relational legalism and self-focused cynicism. But the good news of Jesus can recenter us, recalibrate us—if we will recenter and reorient around *Him*. Gospel centrality best shapes all of our life according to God's Word and empowers us to live lives that serve others best and glorify God the most. Every day of your life, center on the gospel.

It is more important to be kind and helpful than to win

(Becky)

My husband is a professor at a seminary, so we interact with a large number of students at every point along the academic spectrum. Some of them are barely getting by; some of them are eagerly engrossed in doctoral work. Our church in the town neighboring the seminary is filled with many of these students as well, and Jared even leads a residency program through the church for young men training for ministry,

GO OUTSIDE

which also includes many students. So you could accurately say we're surrounded by students most of the time.

I'm grateful to report that the vast majority of these students, no matter how brilliant they are, are also wonderfully winsome, kind, and thoughtful. I actually attend a church where every single pastor is younger than I am, but also more theologically educated. In many ways, they are all smarter than I am, but they use their training and knowledge not to rise above those of us who don't have seminary degrees, but to inform their own lives in ways that help them to teach and lead well the congregation the Lord has entrusted to them. Because of that, I tend to hang on their every word. I'm grateful for the hours they've spent studying and listening to professors and scholars, and I'm eager to let their experiences in classrooms and lecture halls enhance my less-than-formal biblical education.

> If someone speaks about things like love and grace and kindness with no love or grace or kindness in their delivery, we will likely not trust the message.

Unfortunately, however, every now and then we encounter someone whose intelligence is far more developed than their character. Here is my advice about that phenomenon: please, I beg of you, don't be that guy or girl!

I'm so thankful for people who are smarter than me. I greatly enjoy learning (though not so much in a classroom setting), so I am truly grateful to be able to benefit from those who have committed countless hours to reading and studying toward their master of divinity or doctor of philosophy degrees, or whatever other advanced learning they pursue. But no matter how much greater their education, those with advanced learning should speak with respect and kindness. Nobody is interested in hearing from a dismissive, pompous know-it-all. And further, if someone speaks about things like love and grace and kindness with no love or grace or kindness in their delivery, we will likely not trust the message.

I suspect we all see on an almost daily basis people on social media using their intelligence as a club to beat up those who might not have the same credentials they do (but who are often no less intelligent). They wear their degrees and reading lists of extra thick books as badges and permissions to belittle and dismiss. And rather than engage in conversation, they simply state their opinions as though they are irrefutable and anyone in disagreement is of a lesser mind. These are the people who seem much more concerned with advertising their own expertise than with helping others understand theology and doctrine or reason through difficult cultural issues. Frankly, it's a waste of good education.

Here's the thing: it's entirely possible there are many ways the knowledge these people have gained could be so helpful to others, but this is the part that requires wisdom. Knowledge is the retaining of information; wisdom is knowing what to do with it. And there's a big difference between the two.

It's admirable to spend your life learning and growing. It's certainly helpful to take the right approach to studying and to be right in your understanding of whatever you are studying (especially when you're studying Scripture!), but if your "right" views are expressed so arrogantly and dismissively that no one wants to hear them, they are worthless to everyone except you. Or worse, they can be damaging to your position and hurtful to others.

Seek to win more hearts than arguments.

Is it worth it in the long run to win an argument and lose a friend? To win a rhetorical battle but lose an opportunity to share the gospel?

Seek to win more hearts than arguments. Your right views will certainly resonate more deeply and have much greater impact with people who have received your knowledge from a platter full of the fruit of the Spirit.

20.

You are not only as good as what you haven't done

(Jared)

I have saved this chapter for last because it is probably the one thing I wish I'd most known when I was a younger man. If I could get in Doc Brown's DeLorean and go back to talk some sense into my teenage self—but I only had five minutes—I think this is what I would talk to myself about. I would say: "The doctrine of imputation can change your life."

Let me back up a bit.

Ever since I was a little kid, I have had this message playing over and over in my head. It is a voice of accusation, though it sounds just like myself. And it says, "You are only as good as what you haven't done."

This message got reinforced, intentionally by some but inadvertently by most, throughout my life. If I got mostly good grades, I felt it was the bad grade that defined me. If I succeeded athletically, it was my mistakes that overshadowed everything. I felt unapproved, unaccepted, and unloved. Everywhere I went, no matter who I was in relationship with, no matter the good lessons I learned in church, every word got drowned out by the word of disapproval. "You're only as good as what you haven't done."

As you can imagine, this really messed with my sense of spiritual security. It really poisoned my understanding of salvation and discipleship. I believe that I was a believer. I really did trust that God loved me and Jesus died for me. But I felt as though God was kind of holding His nose to love me and that Jesus would take it back if He could. I treated the gospel like a loophole I was exploiting more than a wonderful gift freely and joyfully given to me.

So basically I thought about my Christian life as being defined by my sin and screw-ups. I got in by grace, but I was constantly on thin ice. God was usually disappointed in me. Because I'm only as good as what I haven't done.

When my life fell apart and I went through that period of deep depression, this message got louder and louder in my head. I began to lose hope. But somehow, through God's Spirit, I was reminded of the biblical message of grace all over again. I was startled to discover that the gospel is not just for lost people but also for Christians! I realized for the first time that it was not my sin that defined me and that God wasn't mad at me. No, instead, He has committed Himself to me precisely because He delights in me and has united me eternally and inextricably to His Son. I had discovered the doctrine of the imputation of Christ's righteousness.

This is what imputation means—basically, what someone else has is transferred to you and essentially becomes yours. If I add your name to my checking account and give you full access to use it freely, in essence, I have imputed my money to your account. What I have is considered yours. That's imputation.

Christian theologians often discuss the "double imputation" of the cross of Christ. This means that in His atoning work, Jesus has taken our sin onto Himself as if it is His and at the same time puts His righteousness onto us as if it is ours. This is the great exchange Paul describes in 2 Corinthians 5:21: "He

> He wipes the slate clean in forgiving me of my sins and then inscribes onto that slate the perfect righteousness of His Son.

made the one who did not know sin to be sin for us, so that in him we might become the righteousness of God."

As I said, this vital gospel truth changed my life. Because at the point of my salvation, it wasn't just that God had wiped the slate of my heart clean and then said, "Try again." No, and in fact, if that were the case, it would have taken me a millisecond to tarnish that slate again with my own pride! Instead, He wipes the slate clean in forgiving me of my sins and then inscribes onto that slate the perfect righteousness of His Son.

To be justified, then, is to be forgiven and counted righteous. Jesus' obedience has been imputed to us. And we're no longer as good as what we haven't done. We're no longer as good as what we have done! Instead, we are considered as good as what Christ has done. His obedience is credited to our account as if we'd been the one who carried it out.

If you're a believer in Christ, you need to know that God is not mad at you. He's not disappointed in you. He delights in you always because of what Christ has done. If you have repented of your sin and placed your faith in Jesus, you are clothed in His righteousness. The Son's good works are reckoned your own, and God sees you through the vision of the perfection of Jesus.

This newfound understanding of the gospel for Christians showed me how to grasp the hope I'd been given by Jesus. It helped me drown out the voice of the accuser and the temptations of the flesh in my life. And it strengthened my sense of assurance of salvation and security in heaven. I now have a greater security of my place in heaven—not because I'm great, but because Christ is! And He has covered me in His perfect life forever.

I pray you will find the same riches of grace in this truth too. It will change your life.

Acknowledgments

The seed of this book was planted after a brief talk Becky and I delivered to the Student Leadership at Midwestern Seminary on "Things We Wish We'd Known in Our Twenties." We each chose three topics and alternated speaking on them for about five minutes at a time. So we have to thank Jared Bumpers, Clara Sylvester, and the rest of the seminary Student Leadership team for putting us on this track.

After I tweeted about this talk, it was our friend and Moody Publishers editor Drew Dyck who reached out to ask if we could expand our ideas into a book. So you can thank him for the seed sprouting into what you hold here in your hands.

Becky and I had to feel, in a sense, *authorized* to write a book like this, and we give huge credit to all the young adults at Midwestern Seminary (and its undergrad arm, Spurgeon College) for helping us get there. Their commitment to God's Word and the health of the church has been a huge encouragement to us.

We could say the same about the young adults at Liberty Baptist Church we've had the great privilege to know and counsel over the last eight years. The young people we've hosted in our home, fellowshipped with over meals, and discipled through the Pastoral Training Center are miles and miles spiritually beyond where we were at their age. Their pursuit of personal holiness and desire to see Christ magnified in their lives has helped us reframe our own sense of ministry, particularly in our middle-aged, empty nest years. We are so glad to be "passing the baton," so to speak, to these great young men and women of God.

We also want to thank the little friendship communities in Kansas City, Missouri, and Lancaster, Pennsylvania, that have been so formative and inspiring for our daughters. Their Christian friends past and present have given us a unique picture of "the brethren" and a sweet hope about "the next generation."

Finally, along with Drew Dyck, we want to thank Connor Sterchi and the rest of the Moody team for being wonderful to work with and for shepherding this book to completion.

Thanks also to my—now *our*—literary agent, Don Gates. You're the best.

JARED C. WILSON

Hyper-spiritual approaches to finding God's will don't work. It's time to try something new: Give up.

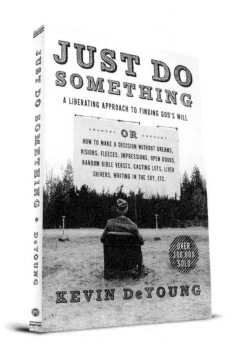

Every twentysomething needs
a little black book of secrets.

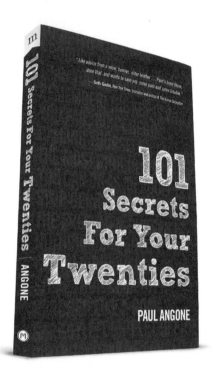

You have been lied to.